초등학생의 영어 친구

리스닝 버디
LISTENING BUDDY

1

리스닝버디 1

지은이	NE능률 영어교육연구소
연구원	한정은, 백수자, 권혜진, 송진아, 황선영
영문 교열	Peter Morton, MyAn Le, Lewis Hugh Hosie
디자인	장현정, 김연주
내지 일러스트	이은교, 전진희, 김현수
내지 사진	www.shutterstock.com
맥편집	ELIM
영업	한기영, 이경구, 박인규, 정철교, 김남준, 김남형, 이우현
마케팅	박혜선, 고유진, 김여진

NE능률이 미래를 그립니다.

교육에 대한 큰 꿈을 품고 시작한 NE능률
처음 품었던 그 꿈을 잊지 않고 40년이 넘는 시간 동안 한 길만을 걸어왔습니다.

이제 NE능률이 앞으로 나아가야 할 길을 그려봅니다.
'평범한 열 개의 제품보다 하나의 탁월한 제품'이라는
변치 않는 철학을 바탕으로 진정한 배움의 가치를 알리는
NE능률이 교육의 미래를 열어가겠습니다.

NE능률   www.neungyule.com

Dear Friends,

I'm your English Buddy!
Forget about all your worries.
I'm here to help you!
Let's smile! Let's learn! And let's have fun!

All the best,
Your English Buddy

★ HOW TO USE ★

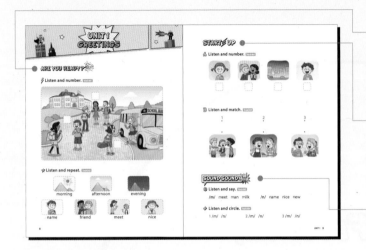

ARE YOU READY

그림을 보면서 본문에서 다룰 주요 단어와 표현을 학습합니다.

START UP

간단한 문제를 통해 학습한 단어와 표현을 확인합니다.

SOUND SOUND

주의해야 할 발음과 억양을 듣고 따라 함으로써 올바른 영어 발음을 익힐 수 있습니다.

LISTEN UP

반복적·단계적으로 구성된 대화를 듣고 연습 문제를 풀어봄으로써, 주요 의사소통 기능을 자연스럽게 습득할 수 있습니다.

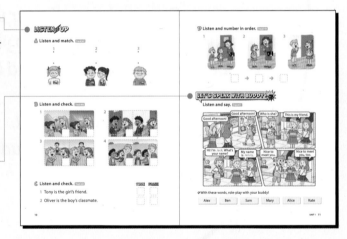

LET'S SPEAK WITH BUDDY

재미있는 만화와 함께 배운 표현들을 복습합니다. 제시된 대체 어휘들을 이용하여 친구와 역할극을 해 봅니다.

DICTATION

앞에서 학습한 내용을 다시 한 번 듣고 받아 써 봅니다. 단어, 문장, 대화 순으로 체계적인 받아쓰기 학습을 할 수 있습니다.

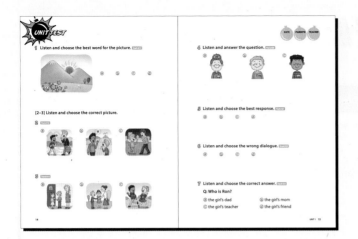

UNIT TEST

해당 Unit에서 배운 내용을 아우르는 다양한
유형의 실전 문제를 통해, 학습한 내용을 충실히
이해했는지 확인할 수 있습니다.

REVIEW TEST

3~4개의 Unit을 학습한 후, 총 10문항으로 구성
된 누적 테스트를 풀어봄으로써 앞서 배운 내용에
대한 성취도를 확인할 수 있습니다.

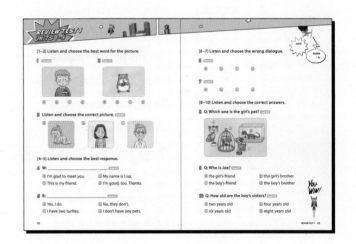

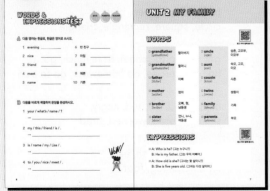

단어장

본책에서 학습한 단어와 표현이 보기 쉽게 정리되어 있습니다.
단어와 표현을 충분히 학습했는지 확인해 볼 수 있도록 간단한
테스트도 함께 제공됩니다.
단어와 표현에 대한 발음은 QR코드를 통해 손쉽게 확인 가능
합니다.

☆ OVERVIEW OF LISTENING BUDDY ☆

Level	Unit	Title	Key Expressions	Key Words
Level 1	1	Greetings	Good morning. How are you? What's your name? This is my friend, Brian.	morning, afternoon, evening, name, friend, meet, nice
	2	My Family	Who is he? How old is she?	grandfather, grandmother, father, mother, brother, sister, uncle, aunt, cousin, twins
	3	Pets	Do you like birds? Do you have any pets?	dog, cat, rabbit, hamster, bird, fish, turtle, lizard
	4	Art Class	What is this/that? What are these/those? Is this/that your glue?	crayon, colored pencil, eraser, sketchbook, glue, scissors, ruler
	5	Music	Can you play the piano? What can you play?	piano, violin, cello, flute, guitar, drums, trumpet
	6	Yummy Food	Do you want some pizza? What do you want?	bread, sandwich, salad, pizza, chicken, noodles, fried rice
	7	Birthday Party	Happy birthday! This is for you. Thank you for coming. Would you like some cake?	card, cake, present, hairpin, robot, backpack, hat
	8	Outdoor Activities	Swim with your brother. Don't ride your bike here. Watch out! / Be careful!	swim, ride, catch, throw, climb up, push, wear
	9	Seven Days	What day is it today? What do you do on Sundays?	Sunday, Monday, Tuesday, Wednesday, Thursday, Friday, Saturday, play soccer, go hiking, have a yoga class, visit my uncle
	10	Weather	How's the weather? / What's the weather like? Let's play soccer outside.	sunny, cloudy, windy, rainy, snowy, hot, cold
Level 2	1	Colors and Shapes	What color is it? What shape is it?	red, yellow, green, blue, circle, square, rectangle, triangle
	2	Everyday Life	What time is it? What time do you go to bed?	get up, go to school, have lunch, go home, exercise, do homework, go to bed
	3	Feelings	How do you feel? Are you scared?	happy, sad, excited, angry, scared, bored, worried, tired
	4	Body Parts	What does it look like? How many eyes does it have?	eye, nose, mouth, ear, arm, hand, leg, foot

Level	Unit	Title	Key Expressions	Key Words
Level 2	5	At Home	Where is my car key?	key, watch, socks, glasses, bed, table, drawer, bookshelf
			Whose socks are these?	
	6	School Subjects	What's your favorite subject?	art, music, English, math, science, P.E., history
			Are you interested in painting?	
	7	Hobbies	What do you like to do in your free time?	listen to music, play tennis, watch movies, take photos, play computer games, do puzzles
			How about playing tennis after school?	
	8	At the Festival	What are they doing?	sing, dance on a stage, look for a restroom, eat snacks, drink soda, watch the fireworks
			Can I drink some soda?	
	9	Cooking	Will you wash the tomatoes?	wash, peel, mix, fry, sweet, salty, sour, spicy
			How does it taste?	
	10	Shopping	I'm looking for a shirt.	shirt, jacket, skirt, pants, shoes, gloves, umbrella
			How much is this skirt?	
			What size do you wear?	
Level 3	1	People Around Me	What does she look like?	tall, short, thin, fat, shy, outgoing, funny, lazy
			What is she like?	
	2	Jobs	What does your father do?	scientist, singer, police officer, firefighter, dentist, pilot, chef, vet
			What do you want to be?	
	3	Four Seasons	Which seasons do you like?	spring, summer, fall, winter, go on a picnic, play at the beach, see colorful leaves, go skiing
			Why do you like summer?	
	4	Sickness	I have a headache.	headache, toothache, stomachache, fever, cough, runny nose, sore throat, see a doctor, take medicine
			You should see a doctor.	
	5	At the Restaurant	Are you ready to order?	order, menu, bill, dessert, steak, hamburger, French fries, pie
			What would you like to have?	
			May I have the bill, please?	
	6	Special Days	What's the date today?	January, February, March, April, May, June, July, August, September, October, November, December, New Year's Day, Earth Day, Halloween, Christmas
			When is your birthday?	
	7	The Past	What did you do yesterday?	played baseball, watched TV, visited a museum, went swimming, had a party, took a trip
			How was your weekend?	
	8	Phone Calls	May I speak to Amy?	answer the phone, hold on, leave a message, call back, hang up, have the wrong number
			Who's calling, please?	
			May I leave a message?	
	9	My Town	Where is the bakery?	library, bank, hospital, bakery, movie theater, turn left, turn right, go straight, next to, between
			How can I get to the movie theater?	
			Go straight and turn left.	
	10	Plans	What are you going to do tomorrow?	go shopping, get a haircut, relax at home, go camping, study Chinese, travel overseas
			Do you have any plans for your vacation?	

★ CONTENTS ★

Let's meet our buddies in Listening Buddy!

Ann   Tom   Jack   Jenny   Kevin

UNIT 1 GREETINGS

ARE YOU READY?

⚡ **Listen and number.** Track 001

⭐ **Listen and repeat.** Track 002

morning

afternoon

evening

name

friend

meet

nice

START UP

A Listen and number. Track 003

B Listen and match. Track 004

1 •

2 •

3 •

•
•
•

SOUND SOUND

⬡ Listen and say. Track 005

/m/ meet man milk   /n/ name nice new

✚ Listen and circle. Track 006

1 /m/ /n/   2 /m/ /n/   3 /m/ /n/

LISTEN UP

A Listen and match. `Track 007`

1   2   3

B Listen and check. `Track 008`

1

2

3

4

C Listen and check. `Track 009`

1 Tony is the girl's friend.

2 Oliver is the boy's classmate.

10

D Listen and number in order. Track 010

1 **2** **3**

☐ → ☐ → ☐

LET'S SPEAK WITH BUDDY

Listen and say. Track 011

✣ With these words, role-play with your buddy!

| Alex | Ben | Sam | Mary | Alice | Kate |

DICTATION

A **Listen and write the letters.** Track 012

1 ___ame

2 m___ ___t

3 ___ ___ ___ning

4 n___ce

5 aftern___ ___n

B **Listen and write the words.** Track 013

1 Good _____!

2 I'm _____, thank you.

3 _____ are you today?

4 This is my _____, Ben.

5 _____ to meet you, too.

| friend | morning | fine | glad | how |

ⓒ Listen and fill in the blanks.

1 Track 014

 : Good _____. How are you?

 : I'm _____. Thank you.

2 Track 015

 : Kate, _____ her name?

 : Her _____ is Grace. She is my friend.

 : Oh, she is pretty.

3 Track 016

 : Hi, Emma. How are you?

 : I'm _____. Thank you.

 : Oh, Ms. Brown, good _____.

This is my _____, Emma.

 : _____ to meet you, Emma.

 : Nice to meet you, too.

UNIT TEST

1 Listen and choose the best word for the picture. Track 017

ⓐ   ⓑ   ⓒ   ⓓ

[2-3] Listen and choose the correct picture.

 Track 018

ⓐ    ⓑ    ⓒ

 Track 019

ⓐ    ⓑ    ⓒ

14

4 Listen and answer the question. Track 020

ⓐ
Gina

ⓑ
Mike

ⓒ
Brian

5 Listen and choose the best response. Track 021

ⓐ   ⓑ   ⓒ   ⓓ

6 Listen and choose the wrong dialogue. Track 022

ⓐ   ⓑ   ⓒ   ⓓ

7 Listen and choose the correct answer. Track 023

Q: Who is Ron?

ⓐ the girl's dad   ⓑ the girl's mom
ⓒ the girl's teacher   ⓓ the girl's friend

UNIT 2
MY FAMILY

ARE YOU READY?

⚡ **Listen and number.** Track 024

☆ **Listen and repeat.** Track 025

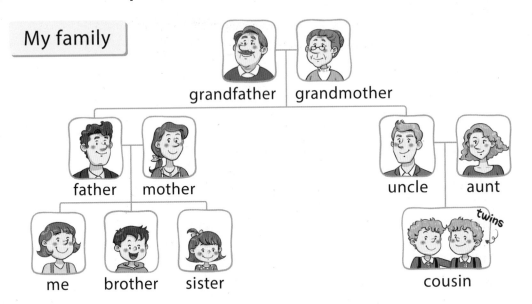

My family

grandfather   grandmother

father   mother   uncle   aunt

me   brother   sister   cousin

twins

STARTE UP

A Listen and number. `Track 026`

B Listen and match. `Track 027`

1
2
3

SOUND SOUND

Listen and say. `Track 028`

/f/ family father four friend

○ Who is he?

○ How old is she?

LISTEN UP

A Listen and match. `Track 029`

1	2	3
He	She	Dan
•	•	•
•	•	•
7 years old	10 years old	12 years old

B Listen and check. `Track 030`

1

2

3

4

C Listen and check. `Track 031`

TRUE FALSE

1 The boy has a sister.

2 The twins are seven years old.

D Listen and number in order. Track 032

☐ → ☐ → ☐

LET'S SPEAK WITH BUDDY

Listen and say. Track 033

✛ Listen again and repeat.

DICTATION

A Listen and write the letters. `Track 034`

1 ___ ___ther

2 aun___

3 ___ather

4 un___ ___ ___

5 ___ ___andmother

B Listen and write the words. `Track 035`

1 He's my _____.

2 _____ are they?

3 How _____ are you?

4 They are my _____.

5 She is my _____.

| old | grandfather | who | sister | cousins |

𝓒 Listen and fill in the blanks.

1 `Track 036`

 : _____ is she?

: She's my _____.

: She's beautiful!

2 `Track 037`

: Josh, who is he?

: He's my _____.

: Do you have any _____ or sisters?

: No, I don't.

3 `Track 038`

 : Who are they?

 : They are my _____ brothers.

 : How _____ are they?

 : They're seven _____ old.

 : Wow. They're so tall!

UNIT TEST

1 Listen and choose the best word for the picture. Track 039

ⓐ   ⓑ   ⓒ   ⓓ

2 Listen and choose the best sentence for the picture. Track 040

ⓐ   ⓑ   ⓒ   ⓓ

3 Listen and choose the correct picture. Track 041

ⓐ    ⓑ    ⓒ

4 Listen and choose the best response. `Track 042`

G: _____

ⓐ   ⓑ   ⓒ   ⓓ

5 Listen and choose the wrong dialogue. `Track 043`

ⓐ   ⓑ   ⓒ   ⓓ

[6–7] Listen and choose the correct answers.

6 Q: Which one is Sue's family? `Track 044`

ⓐ    ⓑ    ⓒ

7 Q: How old is John's cousin? `Track 045`

ⓐ three years old   ⓑ six years old

ⓒ seven years old   ⓓ eleven years old

UNIT 3
PETS

ARE YOU READY?

⚡ **Listen and number.** `Track 046`

☆ **Listen and repeat.** `Track 047`

dog

cat

rabbit

hamster

bird

fish

turtle

lizard

START UP

A Listen and check. `Track 048`

1

2

3

B Listen and match. `Track 049`

1 •

2 •

3 •

•

•

•

SOUND SOUND

⬡ Listen and say. `Track 050`

/r/ rabbit rain run   /l/ lizard lion like

✚ Listen and circle. `Track 051`

1 /r/ /l/   2 /r/ /l/   3 /r/ /l/

LISTEN UP

A Listen and circle. Track 052

1

2

3

B Listen and check. Track 053

1

2

3

4

C Listen and check. Track 054

TRUE   FALSE

1 The girl's mom likes lizards.

2 The boy has two rabbits.

D Listen and mark. Track 055

I have …					
I like …					

LET'S SPEAK WITH BUDDY

Listen and say. Track 056

Do you have any pets?

Yes, I do.

I have three lizards.

Do you like lizards?

Yes! How about you?

I don't like them!

⊕ With these words, role-play with your buddy!

| dogs | cats | hamsters | birds | turtles |

DICTATION

A Listen and write the letters. Track 057

1 c___t

2 fi___ ___

3 r___bb___t

4 ___ ___ ___tle

5 ___i___ard

B Listen and write the words. Track 058

1 Do you have any _____?

2 No, I don't _____ them.

3 Do you have a _____?

4 I like _____ a lot.

5 I have a _____.

| hamsters | dog | bird | pets | like |

ⓒ Listen and fill in the blanks.

1 `Track 059`

 : Do you have any _____?

: Yes, I have two _____.

2 `Track 060`

 : Do you like _____?

 : No, I don't. How about you?

 : I _____ them a lot.

3 `Track 061`

 : Look at the _____!

 : Do you _____ them?

 : Yes, I like lizards a lot.

 : Do you _____ a lizard?

 : No, my mom doesn't like them.

UNIT TEST

1 Listen and choose the best word for the picture. `Track 062`

ⓐ   ⓑ   ⓒ   ⓓ

2 Listen and choose the correct picture. `Track 063`

ⓐ    ⓑ    ⓒ

3 Listen and answer the question. `Track 064`

ⓐ    ⓑ    ⓒ

4 Listen and choose the best response. `Track 065`

ⓐ　　　ⓑ　　　ⓒ　　　ⓓ

5 Listen and choose the wrong dialogue. `Track 066`

ⓐ　　　ⓑ　　　ⓒ　　　ⓓ

[6–7] Listen and choose the correct answers.

6 Q: What is the boy's pet? `Track 067`

ⓐ a bird　　　　　　ⓑ a turtle

ⓒ a lizard　　　　　ⓓ a hamster

7 Q: What does the girl like? `Track 068`

ⓐ cats　　　　　　ⓑ fish

ⓒ rabbits　　　　　ⓓ dogs

[1–2] Listen and choose the best word for the picture.

1 Track 069

ⓐ   ⓑ   ⓒ   ⓓ

2 Track 070

ⓐ   ⓑ   ⓒ   ⓓ

3 Listen and choose the correct picture. Track 071

ⓐ    ⓑ    ⓒ

[4–5] Listen and choose the best response.

4 W: _____ Track 072

ⓐ I'm glad to meet you.   ⓑ My name is Lisa.

ⓒ This is my friend.   ⓓ I'm good, too. Thanks.

5 B: _____ Track 073

ⓐ Yes, I do.   ⓑ No, they don't.

ⓒ I have two turtles.   ⓓ I don't have any pets.

[6–7] Listen and choose the wrong dialogue.

6 Track 074

ⓐ   ⓑ   ⓒ   ⓓ

7 Track 075

ⓐ   ⓑ   ⓒ   ⓓ

[8–10] Listen and choose the correct answers.

8 Q: Which one is the girl's pet? Track 076

9 Q: Who is Joe? Track 077

ⓐ the girl's friend   ⓑ the girl's brother

ⓒ the boy's friend   ⓓ the boy's brother

10 Q: How old are the boy's sisters? Track 078

ⓐ two years old   ⓑ four years old

ⓒ six years old   ⓓ eight years old

YOU WIN!

UNIT 4
ART CLASS

ARE YOU READY?

⚡ **Listen and number.** Track 079

☆ **Listen and repeat.** Track 080

crayon

colored pencil

eraser

sketchbook

glue

scissors

ruler

34

START UP

A Listen and check. Track 081

1

2

3
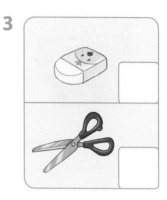

B Listen and match. Track 082

1

2

3

Eric

Tom

Lily

SOUND SOUND

Listen and say. Track 083

/ð/ this that these those

○ What's this? ↗

○ Are these your crayons? ↗

WoW!

LISTEN UP

A Listen and number. Track 084

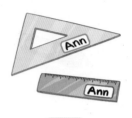

B Listen and check. Track 085

1

2

3

4

C Listen and check. Track 086

TRUE   FALSE

1 The sketchbook is Kate's.

2 They are the boy's scissors.

36

D Listen and write. Track 087

LET'S SPEAK WITH BUDDY

Listen and say. Track 088

➕ Listen again and repeat.

DICTATION

A **Listen and write the letters.** Track 089

1 era___er

2 gl___ ___

3 ___u___er

4 sci___ ___ors

5 col___ ___ed p___ncil

B **Listen and write the words.** Track 090

1 What's _____?

2 They are my _____.

3 Are _____ tigers?

4 Is that your _____?

5 What are _____?

| these | sketchbook | those | crayons | this |

38

C Listen and fill in the blanks.

1 Track 091

: Is _____ your sketchbook?

: Yes, _____ is.

: I have the same one.

2 Track 092

: _____ are those?

: They are my _____.

: Wow, you have a lot.

3 Track 093

: Kate, is this your _____?

: No, it isn't. It's _____.

: Oh, I see. Is that your _____?

: Yes, it's _____.

UNIT TEST

1 Listen and choose the best word for the picture. Track 094

ⓐ   ⓑ   ⓒ   ⓓ

2 Listen and choose the best sentence for the picture. Track 095

ⓐ   ⓑ   ⓒ   ⓓ

3 Listen and choose the correct picture. Track 096

ⓐ    ⓑ    ⓒ

4 **Listen and choose the best response.** Track 097

ⓐ   ⓑ   ⓒ   ⓓ

5 **Listen and choose the wrong dialogue.** Track 098

ⓐ   ⓑ   ⓒ   ⓓ

[6–7] Listen and choose the correct answers.

6 **Q: Which one is the boy's picture?** Track 099

ⓐ    ⓑ    ⓒ

7 **Q: James has _____.** Track 100

ⓐ a crayon   ⓑ crayons

ⓒ a colored pencil   ⓓ colored pencils

UNIT 5 MUSIC

⚡ **Listen and number.** Track 101

☆ **Listen and repeat.** Track 102

piano violin cello flute

guitar drums trumpet

START UP

A Listen and check. `Track 103`

1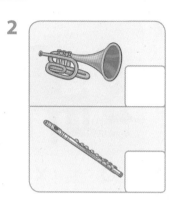

2

3

B Listen and match. `Track 104`

1	2	3
Amy	Sam	Josh

SOUND SOUND

Listen and say. `Track 105`

/v/　violin　very　voice　visit

- Can you play the piano? ↗
- What can you play? ↘

WoW!

LISTEN UP

A Listen and circle. `Track 106`

1

| O | X |

2

| O | X |

3

| O | X |

B Listen and check. `Track 107`

1

2

3

4

C Listen and check. `Track 108`

TRUE FALSE

1 The girl can play the drums.

2 The boy can play the piano and the violin.

Ⓓ Listen and mark. [Track 109]

	🎹	🎻	🎶	🎺	🎸
I can play …					
I can play …					
I can play …					

LET'S SPEAK WITH BUDDY

Listen and say. [Track 110]

☘ With these words, role-play with your buddy!

piano	flute	guitar	drums	trumpet

DICTATION

A Listen and write the letters. `Track 111`

1 ___ello

2 f___ ___te

3 ___ ___ano

4 ___ ___olin

5 g___ ___tar

B Listen and write the words. `Track 112`

1 She can _____ the cello.

2 Can you play the _____?

3 I _____ play the guitar.

4 What _____ you play?

5 He plays the _____ very well.

| can | can't | drums | trumpet | play |

⌒ Listen and fill in the blanks.

1 `Track 113`

: Can she play the _____?

: Yes, she _____. She plays it very well.

: Wow, cool!

2 `Track 114`

: _____ can they play?

: They can play the _____.

: Great!

3 `Track 115`

: Can you play the _____?

: Yes, I can. How about you?

: I can't play the piano, but I can play the _____.

: Nice! We can _____ together.

: Great.

UNIT-TEST

1 Listen and choose the best word for the picture. Track 116

ⓐ   ⓑ   ⓒ   ⓓ

2 Listen and choose the best sentence for the picture. Track 117

ⓐ   ⓑ   ⓒ   ⓓ

3 Listen and choose the correct picture. Track 118

ⓐ    ⓑ    ⓒ

4 **Listen and choose the best response.** `Track 119`

ⓐ   ⓑ   ⓒ   ⓓ

5 **Listen and choose the wrong dialogue.** `Track 120`

ⓐ   ⓑ   ⓒ   ⓓ

[6-7] Listen and choose the correct answers.

6 **Q: What can't the girl play?** `Track 121`

ⓐ    ⓑ    ⓒ

7 **Q: They can play** _____. `Track 122`

ⓐ the violin   ⓑ the cello

ⓒ the piano and the violin   ⓓ the violin and the cello

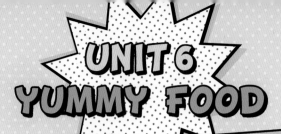

UNIT 6
YUMMY FOOD

ARE YOU READY?

⚡ **Listen and number.** Track 123

⭐ **Listen and repeat.** Track 124

bread

sandwich

salad

pizza

chicken

noodles

fried rice

START UP

A Listen and number. `Track 125`

B Listen and match. `Track 126`

1	2	3
Ben	Sarah	Peter
•	•	•
•	•	•
salad	bread	chicken

Listen and say. `Track 127`

/p/ pizza picture park   /b/ bread breakfast big

Listen and circle. `Track 128`

1 /p/ /b/   2 /p/ /b/   3 /p/ /b/

LISTEN UP

A Listen and circle. Track 129

1

😊 ☹️

2

😊 ☹️

3

😊 ☹️

B Listen and check. Track 130

1

2

3

4

C Listen and check. Track 131

TRUE   FALSE

1 The boy wants some pizza.

☐ ☐

2 The girl doesn't want ice cream.

☐ ☐

D Listen and write. Track 132

1 I want ...

2 I want ...

LET'S SPEAK WITH BUDDY

Listen and say. Track 133

What do you want?

I want some chicken.

Do you want some salad?

Yes, I do.

Do you want some pizza?

Yes, please.

How about noodles?

No, thank you. I'm full.

✚ With these words, role-play with your buddy!

bread | sandwiches | fried rice | fruit | ice cream

DICTATION

A Listen and write the letters. Track 134

1 sal___d

2 ___ ___zza

3 chi___ ___en

4 br___ ___d

5 n___ ___dles

B Listen and write the words. Track 135

1 What do you _____?

2 Do you have some _____?

3 How _____ some ice cream?

4 No, thank you. I'm _____.

5 Do you want a _____?

about   fruit   want   full   sandwich

C Listen and fill in the blanks.

1 `Track 136`

 : Do you want some _____?

: Yes, _____ you.

: Help yourself.

2 `Track 137`

: Dan, what do you _____?

: Do you have pizza and _____?

: Yes, I do. Here you are.

3 `Track 138`

 : Sue, do you want some _____?

 : _____, thank you.

 : Then, how about some _____ _____?

 : Oh, thank you. Do you have some _____, too?

 : Yes, I do. Help yourself.

UNIT TEST

1 Listen and choose the best word or phrase for the picture. [Track 139]

ⓐ   ⓑ   ⓒ   ⓓ

2 Listen and choose the best sentence for the picture. [Track 140]

ⓐ   ⓑ   ⓒ   ⓓ

3 Listen and choose the correct picture. [Track 141]

ⓐ    ⓑ    ⓒ

4 **Listen and choose the best response.** Track 142

G: _____

ⓐ   ⓑ   ⓒ   ⓓ

5 **Listen and choose the wrong dialogue.** Track 143

ⓐ   ⓑ   ⓒ   ⓓ

[6-7] Listen and choose the correct answers.

6 **Q: What does the boy want?** Track 144

ⓐ    ⓑ    ⓒ

7 **Q: What does the girl have?** Track 145

ⓐ bread   ⓑ fried rice

ⓒ salad and noodles   ⓓ pizza and chicken

REVIEW TEST 2
UNITS 4~6

[1–2] Listen and choose the best word for the picture.

1 `Track 146`

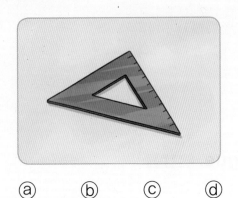

ⓐ   ⓑ   ⓒ   ⓓ

2 `Track 147`

ⓐ   ⓑ   ⓒ   ⓓ

3 Listen and choose the correct picture. `Track 148`

ⓐ

ⓑ

ⓒ

[4–5] Listen and choose the best response.

4 B: _____ `Track 149`

ⓐ No, it's Peter's.   ⓑ Yes, they're mine.

ⓒ It's not my crayon.   ⓓ They're colored pencils.

5 G: _____ `Track 150`

ⓐ Yes, here you are.   ⓑ Yes, I like sandwiches.

ⓒ No, thanks. I'm full.   ⓓ No, I don't like chicken.

[6–7] Listen and choose the wrong dialogue.

6 Track 151

ⓐ   ⓑ   ⓒ   ⓓ

7 Track 152

ⓐ   ⓑ   ⓒ   ⓓ

[8–10] Listen and choose the correct answers.

8 Q: Who is Kate? Track 153

9 Q: The girl has _____. Track 154

ⓐ pencils   ⓑ erasers

ⓒ scissors   ⓓ colored pencils

10 Q: The boy wants some _____. Track 155

ⓐ bread   ⓑ noodles

ⓒ salad   ⓓ fruit

YOU WIN!

ARE YOU READY?

⚡ **Listen and number.** Track 156

☆ **Listen and repeat.** Track 157

card

cake

present

hairpin

robot

backpack

hat

START UP

A Listen and number. Track 158

☐ ☐ ☐ ☐

B Listen and match. Track 159

1 • 2 • 3 •

• • •

SOUND SOUND

◎ Listen and say. Track 160

/æ/ hat cat happy   /ei/ cake make date

✚ Listen and circle. Track 161

1 /æ/ /ei/   2 /æ/ /ei/   3 /æ/ /ei/

LISTEN UP

A Listen and match. Track 162

1

2

3

B Listen and check. Track 163

1

3

2

4

C Listen and check. Track 164

TRUE FALSE

1 The present for Ted is a robot.

2 The boy will have some cake.

D Listen and number in order. Track 165

| 1 | 2 | 3 |

☐ → ☐ → ☐

LET'S SPEAK WITH BUDDY

Listen and say. Track 166

Thank you. Come in.

Happy birthday, Grandma!

Would you like some cake?

Sure, thanks.

This **hairpin** is for you.

You're welcome!

What a surprise! Thank you.

✚ With these words, role-play with your buddy!

| card | robot | backpack | hat | book |

DICTATION

A **Listen and write the letters.** Track 167

1 h___t

2 c___ke

3 pres___nt

4 h___ ___rpin

5 ba___ ___pack

B **Listen and write the words.** Track 168

1 Happy _____!

2 This _____ is for you.

3 What a _____!

4 _____ you for coming.

5 _____ you like some cake?

surprise   birthday   thank   robot   would

C Listen and fill in the blanks.

1 Track 169

 : _____ birthday, Grandma!
This _____ is for you.

: Oh, thank you.

: You're welcome.

2 Track 170

: Thank you for coming to my party.

: Sure. This _____ is for you.

: Oh, thank you. Would you like some _____?

: Yes, please.

3 Track 171

 : Happy birthday, Ted! This _____ is for you.

: What a surprise! What is it?

: Open it.

: Oh, I like this _____. Thanks _____ _____.

: My pleasure.

UNIT TEST

1 **Listen and choose the best word for the picture.** Track 172

ⓐ   ⓑ   ⓒ   ⓓ

2 **Listen and choose the correct picture.** Track 173

ⓐ    ⓑ    ⓒ

3 **Listen and answer the question.** Track 174

ⓐ    ⓑ    ⓒ

4 **Listen and choose the best response.** `Track 175`

ⓐ   ⓑ   ©   ⓓ

5 **Listen and choose the wrong dialogue.** `Track 176`

ⓐ   ⓑ   ©   ⓓ

[6–7] Listen and choose the correct answers.

6 **Q: Which present does Dad give?** `Track 177`

ⓐ    ⓑ    ©

7 **Q: What will the boy's grandma give to him?** `Track 178`

ⓐ robot   ⓑ hat
© cake   ⓓ card

UNIT 8
OUTDOOR ACTIVITIES

ARE YOU READY?

⚡ **Listen and number.** Track 179

☆ **Listen and repeat.** Track 180

swim

ride

catch

throw

climb up

push

wear

START UP

A Listen and number. `Track 181`

B Listen and match. `Track 182`

1   2   3

SOUND SOUND

⬡ Listen and say. `Track 183`

/ʃ/ push wash brush   /tʃ/ catch watch match

✚ Listen and circle. `Track 184`

1 /ʃ/ /tʃ/   2 /ʃ/ /tʃ/   3 /ʃ/ /tʃ/

LISTEN UP

A Listen and number. Track 185

B Listen and check. Track 186

1

2

3

4

C Listen and check. Track 187

	TRUE	FALSE
1 The boy will catch the ball.		
2 The kids will climb up the ladder one by one.		

⒟ Listen and write the numbers. `Track 188`

DOs	DON'Ts
1	

1. wear a cap   2. ride a bike

3. throw a ball   4. swim with friends

LET'S SPEAK WITH BUDDY

Listen and say. `Track 189`

Don't walk! Run!

Okay. I will.

Wait! Don't run so fast. Run with me, please.

✛Listen again and repeat.

DICTATION

A **Listen and write the letters.** Track 190

1 ___ ___row

2 ___ ___im

3 pu___ ___

4 w___ ___r

5 cat___ ___

B **Listen and write the words.** Track 191

1 Don't _____ here.

2 Be _____ next time.

3 Don't _____ your bike here.

4 _____ up the ladder one by one.

5 Don't _____ into the water.

| jump | run | climb | ride | careful |

C Listen and fill in the blanks.

1 Track 192

 : Hey! _____ your helmet.

 : Okay. I _____.

2 Track 193

 : Don't _____ the ball here.

 : Oh, I'm _____.

3 Track 194

 : May I _____ in the pool?

 : Sure. Swim with your _____.

 : Okay. I will.

4 Track 195

 : _____ _____! Don't ride your bike
in the street.

 : Okay. I _____.

 : Don't forget.

UNIT TEST

1 Listen and choose the best word for the picture. Track 196

ⓐ   ⓑ   ⓒ   ⓓ

2 Listen and choose the best sentence for the picture. Track 197

ⓐ   ⓑ   ⓒ   ⓓ

3 Listen and choose the correct picture. Track 198

ⓐ    ⓑ    ⓒ

4 Listen and choose the best response. `Track 199`

W: _____

ⓐ   ⓑ   ⓒ   ⓓ

5 Listen and choose the wrong dialogue. `Track 200`

ⓐ   ⓑ   ⓒ   ⓓ

[6–7] Listen and choose the correct answers.

6 Q: What are they doing? `Track 201`

ⓐ    ⓑ    ⓒ

7 Q: What will the boy do? `Track 202`

ⓐ He will run near the pool.

ⓑ He will climb up the ladder.

ⓒ He will jump into the water.

ⓓ He will swim with his friends.

UNIT 9
SEVEN DAYS

ARE YOU READY?

⚡ **Listen and number.** Track 203

Sun	Mon	Tue	Wed	Thu	Fri	Sat

☆ **Listen and repeat.** Track 204

Sunday	Monday	Tuesday

Wednesday	Thursday	Friday	Saturday

play soccer   go hiking   have a yoga class   visit my uncle

76

START UP

A Listen and check. `Track 205`

1

FRIDAY 3	☐
MONDAY 6	☐

2

SATURDAY 4	☐
SUNDAY 5	☐

3

TUESDAY 7	☐
THURSDAY 9	☐

B Listen and match. `Track 206`

1
•

2
•

3
•

•

•
Tue Wed Thu
7 ① today 8 2 9

•

SOUND SOUND

◉ Listen and say. `Track 207`

Silent D Wednesday handsome sandwich

○ What day is it today? ↘

○ What do you do on Sundays? ↘

LISTEN UP

A Listen and match. `Track 208`

1	2	3
Sun	Thu	Wed

B Listen and check. `Track 209`

1
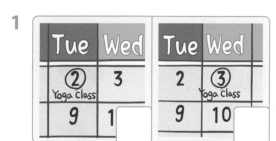

2

3

4

C Listen and check. `Track 210`

TRUE   FALSE

1 The girl visits her uncle on Sundays.

2 The boy plays baseball on Mondays.

ⓓ Listen and write the numbers. `Track 211`

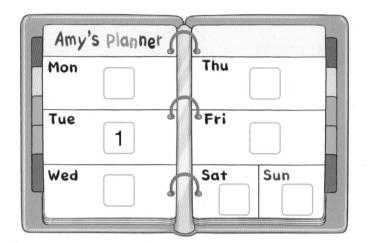

1 have an art class

2 go hiking

3 play the piano

4 visit my aunt

LET'S SPEAK WITH BUDDY

Listen and say. `Track 212`

☙ With these words, role-play with your buddy!

| Sunday | Monday | Tuesday | Wednesday | Thursday | Saturday |

DICTATION

A **Listen and write the letters.** Track 213

1 ___riday

2 M___nday

3 T___ ___ ___day

4 We___ ___esday

5 Sa___ ___ ___day

B **Listen and write the words.** Track 214

1 What _____ is it today?

2 I visit my uncle on _____.

3 What do you do on _____?

4 They go _____ on Saturdays.

5 I play soccer on _____.

Sundays	Thursdays	weekends	day	hiking

C Listen and fill in the blanks.

1 Track 215

 : What does she do on _____?

 : She _____ her grandmother.

2 Track 216

 : What day is it today?

 : It's _____.

 : Oh, I have a _____ _____ today.
I'm late!

3 Track 217

 : _____ _____ is it today?

 : It's Wednesday.

 : What do you do on _____?

 : I play _____ with my friends.

 : Can I join you?

 : Sure.

UNIT TEST

1 Listen and choose the best word for the picture. [Track 218]

ⓐ   ⓑ   ⓒ   ⓓ

2 Listen and choose the best sentence for the picture. [Track 219]

ⓐ   ⓑ   ⓒ   ⓓ

3 Listen and answer the question. [Track 220]

ⓐ    ⓑ    ⓒ

4 Listen and choose the best response. `Track 221`

ⓐ   ⓑ   ⓒ   ⓓ

5 Listen and choose the wrong dialogue. `Track 222`

ⓐ   ⓑ   ⓒ   ⓓ

[6-7] Listen and choose the correct answers.

6 Q: What day is it today? `Track 223`

ⓐ    ⓑ    ⓒ

7 Q: The girl _____ on Thursdays. `Track 224`

ⓐ goes hiking   ⓑ plays soccer

ⓒ has a yoga class   ⓓ visits her grandfather

UNIT 10
WEATHER

ARE YOU READY?

⚡ **Listen and number.** Track 225

☆ **Listen and repeat.** Track 226

sunny

cloudy

windy

rainy

snowy

hot

cold

START UP

A Listen and number. Track 227

B Listen and match. Track 228

1
·
·
2
·
·
3
·
·

SOUND SOUND

Listen and say. Track 229

/ɑː/ hot clock doll hobby

o How's the weather? ↘

o What's the weather like? ↘

LISTEN UP

A Listen and number. `Track 230`

B Listen and check. `Track 231`

1

2

3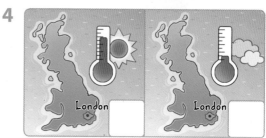

4

C Listen and check. `Track 232`

1 It is very cold and snowy in New York.

2 The boy and his mom will go hiking.

86

⒟ Listen and write. [Track 233]

1 Sue's Diary

2 Joe's Diary

LET'S SPEAK WITH BUDDY

Listen and say. [Track 234]

✛ Listen again and repeat.

DICTATION

A **Listen and write the letters.** Track 235

1 h___t

2 ___indy

3 su___ ___y

4 r___ ___ny

5 cl___ ___dy

B **Listen and write the words.** Track 236

1 How's the _____ today?

2 It's _____.

3 Is it _____?

4 _____ ride our bikes.

5 What's the weather _____?

| cold | like | snowy | let's | weather |

88

C Listen and fill in the blanks.

1 Track 237

: _____ the weather in London?

: It's _____ and cold.

: Oh, dress warmly.

2 Track 238

: What's the weather like today?

: It's _____ but windy.

: Let's _____ _____.

: No, let's not.

3 Track 239

: Sue, how's the weather today?

: It's sunny and _____.

: Let's _____ _____.

: Sorry, but I can't swim. How about riding our bikes?

: Sounds _____.

UNIT TEST

1 Listen and choose the best word for the picture. `Track 240`

ⓐ　　　ⓑ　　　ⓒ　　　ⓓ

2 Listen and choose the best sentence for the picture. `Track 241`

ⓐ　　　ⓑ　　　ⓒ　　　ⓓ

3 Listen and choose the correct picture. `Track 242`

ⓐ 　　ⓑ 　　ⓒ

4 Listen and choose the best response. `Track 243`

ⓐ   ⓑ   ⓒ   ⓓ

5 Listen and choose the wrong dialogue. `Track 244`

ⓐ   ⓑ   ⓒ   ⓓ

[6–7] Listen and choose the correct answers.

6 Q: What will they do? `Track 245`

ⓐ    ⓑ    ⓒ

7 Q: How's the weather in London? `Track 246`

ⓐ sunny but cold   ⓑ sunny but windy

ⓒ cloudy and cold   ⓓ cloudy and windy

[1–2] Listen and choose the best word for the picture.

1 Track 247

ⓐ   ⓑ   ⓒ   ⓓ

2 Track 248

ⓐ   ⓑ   ⓒ   ⓓ

3 Listen and choose the correct picture. Track 249

ⓐ    ⓑ    ⓒ

[4–5] Listen and choose the best response.

4 G: _____ Track 250

  ⓐ Yes, it is.   ⓑ It's Wednesday.

  ⓒ You're very busy.   ⓓ I go hiking on Fridays.

5 B: _____ Track 251

  ⓐ Yes, it's windy.   ⓑ Sorry. I'm tired.

  ⓒ No, it's cool.   ⓓ That's a good idea.

[6–7] Listen and choose the wrong dialogue.

6 `Track 252`

    ⓐ   ⓑ   ⓒ   ⓓ

7 `Track 253`

    ⓐ   ⓑ   ⓒ   ⓓ

[8–10] Listen and choose the correct answers.

8 Q: Where does the boy live? `Track 254`

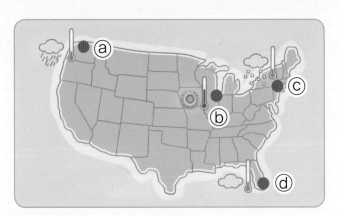

9 Q: The girl will _____. `Track 255`

   ⓐ run fast   ⓑ ride a bike in the street

   ⓒ wear a helmet   ⓓ climb up the ladder

10 Q: The boy _____ on Sundays. `Track 256`

   ⓐ plays baseball   ⓑ has an art class

   ⓒ goes hiking   ⓓ visits his uncle

You WIN!

지은이

NE능률 영어교육연구소

NE능률 영어교육연구소는 혁신적이며 효율적인 영어 교재를 개발하고
영어 학습의 질을 한 단계 높이고자 노력하는 NE능률의 연구조직입니다.

리스닝버디 1

펴 낸 이	주민홍
펴 낸 곳	서울특별시 마포구 월드컵북로 396(상암동) 누리꿈스퀘어 비즈니스타워 10층
	(주)NE능률 (우편번호 03925)
펴 낸 날	2016년 1월 5일 개정판 제1쇄
	2021년 10월 15일 제10쇄
전 화	02 2014 7114
팩 스	02 3142 0356
홈페이지	www.neungyule.com
등록번호	제 1-68호
I S B N	979-11-253-0972-7 63740
정 가	13,000원

NE 능률

고객센터

교재 내용 문의 : contact.nebooks.co.kr (별도의 가입 절차 없이 작성 가능)
제품 구매, 교환, 불량, 반품 문의 : 02-2014-7114
☎ 전화문의는 본사 업무시간 중에만 가능합니다.

NE능률 교재 MAP

아래 교재 MAP을 참고하여 본인의 현재 혹은 목표 수준에 따라 교재를 선택하세요.
NE능률 교재들과 함께 영어실력을 쑥쑥~ 올려보세요!
MP3 등 교재 부가 학습 서비스 및 자세한 교재 정보는 www.nebooks.co.kr 에서 확인하세요.

듣기
말하기
쓰기

초1-2	초3	초3-4	초4-5	초5-6
	리스닝버디 1	리스닝버디 2	리스닝버디 3	초등영어 Listening Tutor Intermediate 1,2,3
		초등영어 Listening Tutor Beginner 1,2,3	능률 초등영어 듣기모의고사 10회 5-1, 5-2	능률 초등영어 듣기모의고사 10회 6-1, 6-2
		능률 초등영어 듣기모의고사 10회 4-1, 4-2		

초6-예비중	중1	중1-2	중2-3	중3
Writing Builder 1	1316팬클럽 듣기 1	1316팬클럽 듣기 2	Junior Listening Expert 3	1316팬클럽 듣기 3
	능률중학영어듣기 모의고사 22회 1	능률중학영어듣기 모의고사 22회 2	Writing Builder 3	능률중학영어듣기 모의고사 22회 3
	Junior Listening Expert 1	Junior Listening Expert 2	쓰기로 마스터하는 중학서술형 2학년	Junior Listening Expert 4
	Writing Builder 2			쓰기로 마스터하는 중학서술형 3학년
	쓰기로 마스터하는 중학서술형 1학년			

중3-예비고	고1	고1-2	고2-3	고3
	TEPS BY STEP L+V Basic		TEPS BY STEP L+V 1	

수능 이상/ 토플 80-89 · 텝스 600-699점	수능 이상/ 토플 90-99 · 텝스 700-799점	수능 이상/ 토플 100 · 텝스 800점 이상		
TEPS BY STEP L+V 2	RADIX TOEFL Black Label Listening 1	TEPS BY STEP L+V 3		
RADIX TOEFL Blue Label Listening 1		RADIX TOEFL Black Label Listening 2		
RADIX TOEFL Blue Label Listening 2				

초등학생의 영어 친구

리스닝 버디

정답 및 해석

HA! HA! HA!

1

NE 능률

초등학생의 영어 친구

리스닝 버디

정답 및 해석

1

UNIT 1 GREETINGS

ANSWERS

P.8

P.9

START UP

A Listen and number.

3 2 1 4

B Listen and match.

SOUND SOUND

🎧 Listen and say.

/m/ meet man milk /n/ name nice new

✏ Listen and circle.

1 (m)/ /n/ 2 /m/ (n)/ 3 /m/ (n)/

UNIT 1 9

P.10

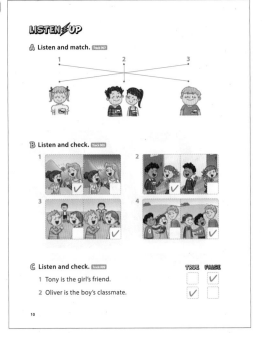

P.11

P.12~13 **DICTATION**

A 1 n   2 e, e   3 e, v, e
   4 i   5 o, o

B 1 morning 2 fine   3 How
   4 friend   5 Glad

2

C 1 evening, fine
  2 what's, name
  3 good, afternoon, friend, Nice

P.14~15 UNIT TEST

1 ⓐ 2 ⓒ 3 ⓐ 4 ⓑ
5 ⓒ 6 ⓓ 7 ⓓ

SCRIPTS & 해석

P.8 ARE YOU READY?

⚡ Listen and number.
  1 G1: Good morning, Kate. How are you?
      (안녕, Kate. 어떻게 지내니?)
    G2: I'm fine. Thanks. (난 잘 지내. 고마워.)

  2 G: Hi, what's your name?
      (안녕, 네 이름은 뭐니?)
    B: I'm Joe. (난 Joe야.)

  3 G: Henry, this is my friend, Brian.
      (Henry, 얘는 내 친구 Brian이야.)
    B: Nice to meet you. (만나서 반가워.)

⭐ Listen and repeat.
morning (아침)   afternoon (오후)   evening (저녁)
name (이름)   friend (친구)   meet (만나다)
nice (좋은, 즐거운)

P.9 START UP

Ⓐ Listen and number.
  1 evening (저녁)
  2 friend (친구)
  3 name (이름)
  4 nice (좋은, 즐거운)

Ⓑ Listen and match.
  1 G: This is my friend, Ben. (얘는 내 친구 Ben이야.)
    B: Nice to meet you. (만나서 반가워.)

  2 B: What's your name? (네 이름은 뭐니?)
    G: My name is Lisa. (내 이름은 Lisa야.)

  3 B: Good evening. How are you?
      (안녕. 어떻게 지내니?)
    G: I'm fine. Thank you. (난 잘 지내. 고마워.)

P.9 SOUND SOUND

🄾 Listen and say.
/m/ meet (만나다)   man (남자)   milk (우유)
/n/ name (이름)   nice (좋은, 즐거운) new (새로운)

➕ Listen and circle.
  1 milk   2 new   3 nice

P.10~11 LISTEN UP

Ⓐ Listen and match.
  1 G: What's his name? (그의 이름은 뭐니?)
    B: His name is Alex. (그의 이름은 Alex야.)

  2 G: What are their names? (그들의 이름은 뭐니?)
    B: They are Tom and Linda.
      (그들은 Tom과 Linda야.)

  3 G: What's her name? (그녀의 이름은 뭐니?)
    B: She is Mary. (그녀는 Mary야.)

Ⓑ Listen and check.
  1 W: Good morning, Alice. How are you today?
      (안녕, Alice. 오늘 기분 어떠니?)
    G: I'm good, thank you. And you?
      (전 좋아요, 고맙습니다. 당신은요?)
    W: I'm good, too. Thanks. (나도 좋아. 고마워.)

  2 B: Good afternoon. (안녕.)
    G: Good afternoon. What's your name?
      (안녕. 네 이름은 뭐니?)
    B: I'm Eric. (난 Eric이야.)

  3 B: Kate, what's her name?
      (Kate, 그녀의 이름은 뭐니?)
    G: Her name is Grace. She is my friend.
      (그녀의 이름은 Grace야. 그녀는 내 친구야.)
    B: Oh, she is pretty. (오, 그녀는 예쁘구나.)

  4 B: Dad, this is my friend, Sally.
      (아빠, 얘는 제 친구 Sally예요.)
    M: Nice to meet you, Sally.
      (만나서 반갑구나, Sally.)
    G: Nice to meet you, too. (저도 만나서 반가워요.)

Ⓒ Listen and check.
  1 G: Hi, Henry. How are you?
      (안녕, Henry. 어떻게 지내니?)
    B1: Good, thanks. This is my friend, Tony.
      (잘 지내, 고마워. 얘는 내 친구 Tony야.)

3

G: Hi, Tony. I'm glad to meet you.
(안녕, Tony. 만나서 반가워.)

B2: I'm glad to meet you, too.
(나도 만나서 반가워.)

Question: Tony is the girl's friend.
(Tony는 소녀의 친구이다.)

2 **W:** Hi, Ron! (안녕, Ron!)

B: Hello, Grandma! These are my classmates.
(안녕하세요, 할머니! 얘들은 제 반 친구들이에요.)

W: What are their names? (그들의 이름은 뭐니?)

B: This is Oliver, and this is Albert.
(얘는 Oliver이고, 얘는 Albert예요.)

W: Glad to meet you. (만나서 반갑구나.)

Question: Oliver is the boy's classmate.
(Oliver는 소년의 반 친구이다.)

Listen and number in order.

B: Hi, Emma. How are you?
(안녕, Emma. 어떻게 지내니?)

G: I'm good. Thank you. (난 잘 지내. 고마워.)

B: Oh, Ms. Brown, good morning. This is my friend, Emma.
(오, Brown 선생님, 안녕하세요. 얘는 제 친구 Emma예요.)

W: Nice to meet you, Emma.
(만나서 반갑구나, Emma.)

G: Nice to meet you, too. (저도 만나서 반가워요.)

P.11 **LET'S SPEAK WITH BUDDY**

Listen and say.

Ann: Good afternoon! (안녕!)
Jack: Good afternoon! (안녕!)

Jack: Who is she? (그녀는 누구니?)
Ann: This is my friend. (얘는 내 친구야.)

Jack: Hi! I'm Jack. What's your name?
(안녕, 난 Jack이야. 네 이름은 뭐니?)
Jenny: My name is Jenny. (내 이름은 Jenny야.)

Jack: Nice to meet you. (만나서 반가워.)
Jenny: Nice to meet you, too. (나도 만나서 반가워.)

P.12~13 **DICTATION**

1 name (이름)
2 meet (만나다)
3 evening (저녁)

4 nice (좋은, 즐거운)
5 afternoon (오후)

1 Good morning! (안녕!)
2 I'm fine, thank you. (난 잘 지내, 고마워.)
3 How are you today? (오늘 기분 어떠니?)
4 This is my friend, Ben. (얘는 내 친구 Ben이야.)
5 Glad to meet you, too. (나도 만나서 반가워.)

1 **B:** Good evening. How are you?
(안녕. 어떻게 지내니?)
G: I'm fine. Thank you. (난 잘 지내. 고마워.)

2 **B:** Kate, what's her name?
(Kate, 그녀의 이름은 뭐니?)
G: Her name is Grace. She is my friend.
(그녀의 이름은 Grace야. 그녀는 내 친구야.)
B: Oh, she is pretty. (오, 그녀는 예쁘구나.)

3 **B:** Hi, Emma. How are you?
(안녕, Emma. 어떻게 지내니?)
G: I'm good. Thank you. (난 잘 지내. 고마워.)
B: Oh, Ms. Brown, good afternoon. This is my friend, Emma.
(오, Brown 선생님, 안녕하세요. 얘는 제 친구 Emma예요.)
W: Nice to meet you, Emma.
(만나서 반갑구나, Emma.)
G: Nice to meet you, too. (저도 만나서 반가워요.)

P.14~15 **UNIT TEST**

1 ⓐ morning (아침)   ⓑ friend (친구)
ⓒ evening (저녁)   ⓓ meet (만나다)

2 **M:** Good evening. How are you?
(안녕. 어떻게 지내니?)
B: I'm fine. Thank you. (전 잘 지내요. 고맙습니다.)

3 **B:** Mom, this is my friend, Lisa.
(엄마, 얘는 제 친구 Lisa예요.)
W: Nice to meet you, Lisa. (만나서 반갑구나, Lisa.)
G: Nice to meet you, too. (저도 만나서 반가워요.)

4 **G:** Hi, I'm Gina. What's your name?
(안녕, 난 Gina야. 네 이름은 뭐니?)
B: My name is Mike. (내 이름은 Mike야.)

Question: What's the boy's name?
(소년의 이름은 무엇인가?)

5 **W:** What's his name? (그의 이름은 뭐니?)
ⓐ I'm fine, thanks. (난 잘 지내, 고마워.)

4

ⓑ I'm Sally. (난 Sally야.)

ⓒ His name is Ben. (그의 이름은 Ben이야.)

ⓓ I'm glad to meet you. (만나서 반가워.)

6 ⓐ **G**: What's your name? (네 이름은 뭐니?)

    B: I'm Henry. (난 Henry야.)

  ⓑ **G**: How are you? (어떻게 지내니?)

    B: I'm good. Thanks. (난 잘 지내. 고마워.)

  ⓒ **G**: Nice to meet you. (만나서 반가워.)

    B: Nice to meet you, too. (나도 만나서 반가워.)

  ⓓ **G**: What are their names? (그들의 이름은 뭐니?)

    B: They're friends. (그들은 친구야.)

7 **G**: Dad, this is my friend, Ron. Ron, this is my dad.
    (아빠, 얘는 제 친구 Ron이에요. Ron, 이분은 우리 아빠
    셔.)

  M: I'm glad to meet you, Ron.
    (만나서 반갑구나, Ron.)

  B: I'm glad to meet you, too. (저도 만나서 반가워요.)

Question: Who is Ron? (Ron은 누구인가?)

UNIT 2 MY FAMILY

ANSWERS

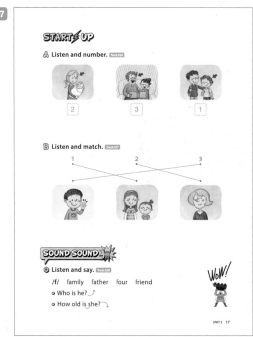

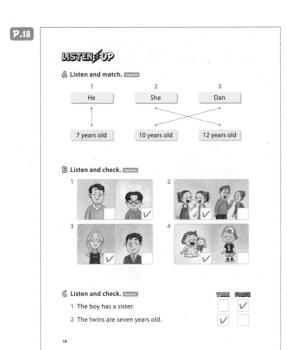

C
1 Who, mother
2 cousin, brothers
3 twin, old, years

P.22~23 **UNIT TEST**

1 ⓓ   2 ⓒ   3 ⓑ   4 ⓑ
5 ⓓ   6 ⓐ   7 ⓒ

SCRIPTS & 해석

P.16 **ARE YOU READY?**

⚡ **Listen and number.**
1 **G**: Who is he? (그는 누구니?)
  B: He is my father. (그는 우리 아빠야.)

2 **G**: How old is she? (그녀는 몇 살이니?)
  B: She is five years old. (그녀는 다섯 살이야.)

☆ **Listen and repeat.**
grandfather (할아버지)   grandmother (할머니)
father (아빠)   mother (엄마)
brother (오빠, 형, 남동생)   sister (언니, 누나, 여동생)
uncle (삼촌, 고모부, 이모부)   aunt (숙모, 고모, 이모)
cousin (사촌)   twins (쌍둥이)

P.17 **START UP**

A **Listen and number.**
1 brother (남동생)
2 mother (엄마)
3 grandfather (할아버지)

B **Listen and match.**
1 **B**: Who are they? (그들은 누구니?)
  G: They are my sisters. (그들은 내 여동생들이야.)

2 **B**: Who is she? (그녀는 누구니?)
  G: She is my aunt. (그녀는 우리 이모야.)

3 **B**: How old is he? (그는 몇 살이니?)
  G: He is four years old. (그는 네 살이야.)

P.17 **SOUND SOUND**

⬡ **Listen and say.**
/f/ family (가족)   father (아빠)

P.20~21 **DICTATION**

A 1 m, o   2 t   3 f
     4 c, l, e   5 g, r

B 1 grandfather   2 Who   3 old
     4 cousins   5 sister

four (4, 넷)   friend (친구)
- Who is he? (그는 누구니?)
- How old is she? (그녀는 몇 살이니?)

P.18~19 **LISTEN UP**

Ⓐ **Listen and match.**

1 G: How old is he? (그는 몇 살이니?)
   B: He's seven years old. (그는 일곱 살이야.)

2 G: How old is she? (그녀는 몇 살이니?)
   B: She's twelve years old. (그녀는 열두 살이야.)

3 G: Dan, how old are you? (Dan, 너는 몇 살이니?)
   B: I'm ten years old. (나는 열 살이야.)

Ⓑ **Listen and check.**

1 G: This is my brother. (얘는 내 남동생이야.)
   B: How old is he? (그는 몇 살이니?)
   G: He's eight years old. (그는 여덟 살이야.)

2 B: Who are they? (그들은 누구니?)
   G: They're my cousins. They're twins.
      (그들은 내 사촌들이야. 그들은 쌍둥이야.)

3 G: Who is she? (그녀는 누구니?)
   B: She's my mother. (그녀는 우리 엄마야.)
   G: She's beautiful! (아름다우시다!)

4 B: This is my baby sister.
      (얘는 내 아기 여동생이야.)
   G: What a cute girl! How old is she?
      (정말 귀여운 소녀구나! 그녀는 몇 살이니?)
   B: She's two years old. (그녀는 두 살이야.)

Ⓒ **Listen and check.**

1 G: Josh, who is he? (Josh, 그는 누구니?)
   B: He's my cousin. (그는 내 사촌이야.)
   G: Do you have any brothers or sisters?
      (너는 형제나 자매가 있니?)
   B: No, I don't. (아니, 없어.)

   Question: The boy has a sister.
            (소년은 여자 형제가 있다.)

2 G: Who are they? (그들은 누구니?)
   B: They are my twin brothers.
      (그들은 내 쌍둥이 남동생들이야.)
   G: How old are they? (그들은 몇 살이니?)
   B: They're seven years old. (그들은 일곱 살이야.)
   G: Wow. They're so tall! (와. 키가 정말 크구나!)

Question: The twins are seven years old.
         (쌍둥이는 일곱 살이다.)

Ⓓ **Listen and number in order.**

B: Look at these photos. (이 사진들 좀 봐.)
G: Wow! Who are they? (와! 저분들은 누구시니?)
B: They are my grandfather and grandmother.
   (그들은 우리 할아버지와 할머니야.)
G: They look nice. (멋져 보이신다.)
B: Here are my parents and my sister.
   (여기는 우리 부모님과 여동생이야.)
G: Then, who is that? (그럼, 쟤는 누구야?)
B: That's me! I was five years old then.
   (그건 나야! 그때 난 다섯 살이었어.)

P.19 **LET'S SPEAK WITH BUDDY**

◉ **Listen and say.**

Tom: Who is he? (쟤는 누구니?)

Ann: He's my brother. (그는 내 남동생이야.)

Tom: How old is he? (그는 몇 살이니?)
Ann: He's five years old. (다섯 살이야.)

Tom: How cute! (정말 귀엽다!)

P.20~21 **DICTATION**

Ⓐ 1 mother (엄마)
   2 aunt (숙모, 고모, 이모)
   3 father (아빠)
   4 uncle (삼촌, 고모부, 이모부)
   5 grandmother (할머니)

Ⓑ 1 He's my grandfather. (그는 우리 할아버지야.)
   2 Who are they? (그들은 누구니?)
   3 How old are you? (너는 몇 살이니?)
   4 They are my cousins. (그들은 내 사촌들이야.)
   5 She is my sister. (그녀는 우리 누나야.)

Ⓒ 1 G: Who is she? (그녀는 누구니?)
      B: She's my mother. (그녀는 우리 엄마야.)
      G: She's beautiful! (아름다우시다!)

   2 G: Josh, who is he? (Josh, 그는 누구니?)
      B: He's my cousin. (그는 내 사촌이야.)
      G: Do you have any brothers or sisters?
         (너는 형제나 자매가 있니?)
      B: No, I don't. (아니, 없어.)

3 **G**: Who are they? (그들은 누구니?)
   B: They are my twin brothers.
      (그들은 내 쌍둥이 남동생들이야.)
   G: How old are they? (그들은 몇 살이니?)
   B: They're seven years old. (그들은 일곱 살이야.)
   G: Wow. They're so tall! (와. 키가 정말 크구나!)

P.22-23 UNIT TEST

1 ⓐ father (아빠)
   ⓑ mother (엄마)
   ⓒ grandfather (할아버지)
   ⓓ grandmother (할머니)

2 ⓐ She's my mother. (그녀는 우리 엄마이다.)
   ⓑ She's my aunt. (그녀는 우리 이모이다.)
   ⓒ She's my baby sister. (그녀는 내 아기 여동생이다.)
   ⓓ She's my grandmother. (그녀는 우리 할머니이다.)

3 **G**: Who are they? (그들은 누구니?)
   B: They are my brothers. They are twins.
      (그들은 내 남동생들이야. 그들은 쌍둥이야.)
   G: How cute! (귀엽다!)

4 **B**: Do you have any brothers or sisters?
      (너는 형제나 자매가 있니?)
   G: No, I don't. (아니, 없어.)
   B: Then, who is he? (그럼, 그는 누구니?)
   G: _____
   ⓐ He's my brother. (그는 우리 오빠야.)
   ⓑ He's my cousin. (그는 내 사촌이야.)
   ⓒ He's five years old. (그는 다섯 살이야.)
   ⓓ He's cute. (그는 귀여워.)

5 ⓐ **G**: Who are they? (그들은 누구니?)
      B: They are my family. (그들은 우리 가족이야.)
   ⓑ **G**: How old are you? (너는 몇 살이니?)
      B: I'm eleven years old. (나는 열한 살이야.)
   ⓒ **G**: Who is she? (그녀는 누구니?)
      B: She's my twin sister.
         (그녀는 내 쌍둥이 여동생이야.)
   ⓓ **G**: How old is he? (그는 몇 살이니?)
      B: He's my uncle. (그는 우리 삼촌이야.)

6 **B**: Sue, who are they? (Sue, 그들은 누구니?)
   G: They are my mother and father.
      (그들은 우리 엄마와 아빠야.)
   B: Do you have any brothers or sisters?
      (너는 형제나 자매가 있니?)
   G: No, I don't. (아니, 없어.)

Question: Which one is Sue's family?
      (어느 것이 Sue의 가족인가?)

7 **G**: Hi, John! Who is she? (안녕, John! 그녀는 누구니?)
   B: She's my cousin. (그녀는 내 사촌이야.)
   G: How old is she? (그녀는 몇 살이니?)
   B: She's seven years old. (그녀는 일곱 살이야.)

Question: How old is John's cousin?
      (John의 사촌은 몇 살인가?)

UNIT 3 PETS

ANSWERS

P.24

P.25

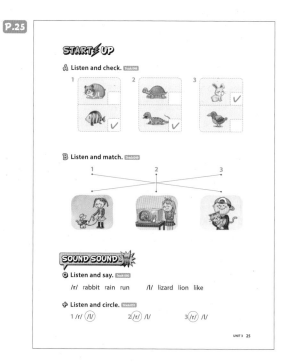

P.26

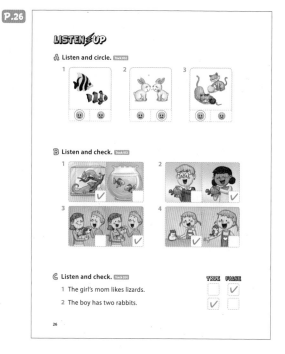

P.27

P.28~29 DICTATION

A 1 a 2 s, h 3 a, i
4 t, u, r 5 l, z

B 1 pets 2 like 3 bird
4 hamsters 5 dog

C 1 pets, dogs
　2 turtles, like
　3 lizards, like, have

UNIT TEST
　1 ⓑ　2 ⓐ　3 ⓑ　4 ⓑ
　5 ⓓ　6 ⓒ　7 ⓒ

SCRIPTS & 해석

ARE YOU READY?

⚡ **Listen and number.**
　1 B: Do you like birds? (너는 새를 좋아하니?)
　　G: Yes, I do! (응, 좋아해!)

　2 G: What a cute dog! (정말 귀여운 개구나!)
　　B: Thanks. Do you have any pets?
　　　(고마워. 너는 애완동물을 기르니?)
　　G: Yes, I have a cat.
　　　(응, 나는 고양이 한 마리를 길러.)

☆ **Listen and repeat.**
　dog (개)　　　cat (고양이)　　　rabbit (토끼)
　hamster (햄스터)　bird (새)　　　fish (물고기)
　turtle (거북이)　lizard (도마뱀)

START UP

Ⓐ **Listen and check.**
　1 fish (물고기)
　2 lizard (도마뱀)
　3 rabbit (토끼)

Ⓑ **Listen and match.**
　1 G: Do you have a dog? (너는 개를 기르니?)
　　B: No, I don't. I have a cat.
　　　(아니, 기르지 않아. 나는 고양이 한 마리를 길러.)

　2 B: Do you like hamsters?
　　　(너는 햄스터를 좋아하니?)
　　G: No, I don't like them.
　　　(아니, 나는 햄스터를 좋아하지 않아.)

　3 B: Do you have any pets?
　　　(너는 애완동물을 기르니?)
　　G: Yes, I have two dogs.
　　　(응, 나는 개 두 마리를 길러.)

SOUND SOUND

◉ **Listen and say.**
　/r/ rabbit (토끼)　rain (비)　　run (달리다)
　/l/ lizard (도마뱀)　lion (사자)　like (좋아하다)

✚ **Listen and circle.**
　1 like　2 run　3 rain

LISTEN UP

Ⓐ **Listen and circle.**
　1 B: Do you like fish? (너는 물고기를 좋아하니?)
　　G: Yes, I do. (응, 좋아해.)

　2 B: Do you like rabbits? (너는 토끼를 좋아하니?)
　　G: No, I don't. (아니, 좋아하지 않아.)

　3 B: Do you like cats? (너는 고양이를 좋아하니?)
　　G: Yes, I like them. (응, 나는 고양이를 좋아해.)

Ⓑ **Listen and check.**
　1 B: Do you have any pets?
　　　(너는 애완동물을 기르니?)
　　G: Yes, I have two lizards.
　　　(응, 나는 도마뱀 두 마리를 길러.)
　　B: Oh, I like lizards! (오, 나는 도마뱀을 좋아해!)
　2 G: Do you like turtles? (너는 거북이를 좋아하니?)
　　B: No, I don't. How about you?
　　　(아니, 좋아하지 않아. 너는 어때?)
　　G: I like them a lot. (나는 거북이를 많이 좋아해.)
　3 B: What a cute cat! (정말 귀여운 고양이구나!)
　　G: Thanks. Do you have any pets?
　　　(고마워. 너는 애완동물을 기르니?)
　　B: Yes, I have a dog. (응, 나는 개 한 마리를 길러.)
　4 B: Do you like birds? (너는 새를 좋아하니?)
　　G: No, I don't like them. But I like hamsters.
　　　(아니, 나는 새를 좋아하지 않아. 하지만 나는 햄스터를 좋아해.)

Ⓒ **Listen and check.**
　1 G: Look at the lizards! (도마뱀 좀 봐!)
　　B: Do you like them? (너는 도마뱀을 좋아하니?)
　　G: Yes, I like lizards a lot.
　　　(응, 나는 도마뱀을 많이 좋아해.)
　　B: Do you have a lizard? (너는 도마뱀을 기르니?)
　　G: No, my mom doesn't like them.
　　　(아니, 엄마가 도마뱀을 좋아하지 않으셔.)

　　Question: The girl's mom likes lizards.
　　　　　　　(소녀의 엄마는 도마뱀을 좋아한다.)

10

2 **B:** Do you have a dog? (너는 개를 기르니?)

   G: No, I don't have any pets. How about you?

      (아니, 나는 애완동물을 기르지 않아. 너는 어때?)

   B: I don't have a dog. But I have two rabbits.

      (나는 개를 기르지 않아. 하지만 토끼 두 마리를 길러.)

   Question: The boy has two rabbits.

           (소년은 토끼 두 마리를 기른다.)

D **Listen and mark.**

  G: Do you have a bird? (너는 새를 기르니?)

  B: No, but I have a turtle and a fish. How about you, Lily?

    (아니, 하지만 나는 거북이 한 마리와 물고기 한 마리를 길러. 너는 어때, Lily?)

  G: I don't have any pets. But I like rabbits and cats.

    (나는 애완동물을 기르지 않아. 하지만 나는 토끼와 고양이를 좋아해.)

  B: Oh, I like rabbits, too. (오, 나도 토끼를 좋아해.)

P.27 **LET'S SPEAK WITH BUDDY**

● **Listen and say.**

  Tom: Do you have any pets?

    (너는 애완동물을 기르니?)

  Jenny: Yes, I do. (응, 길러.)

  Jenny: I have three lizards.

    (나는 도마뱀 세 마리를 길러.)

  Tom: Do you like lizards? (너는 도마뱀을 좋아하니?)

  Jenny: Yes! How about you? (응! 너는 어때?)

  Tom: I don't like them! (나는 도마뱀을 좋아하지 않아!)

P.28~29 **DICTATION**

A 1 cat (고양이)

  2 fish (물고기)

  3 rabbit (토끼)

  4 turtle (거북이)

  5 lizard (도마뱀)

B 1 Do you have any pets? (너는 애완동물을 기르니?)

  2 No, I don't like them.

    (아니, 나는 그것들을 좋아하지 않아.)

  3 Do you have a bird? (너는 새를 기르니?)

  4 I like hamsters a lot. (나는 햄스터를 많이 좋아해.)

  5 I have a dog. (나는 개 한 마리를 길러.)

C 1 **B:** Do you have any pets?

    (너는 애완동물을 기르니?)

   G: Yes, I have two dogs.

    (응, 나는 개 두 마리를 길러.)

  2 **G:** Do you like turtles? (너는 거북이를 좋아하니?)

   B: No, I don't. How about you?

    (아니, 좋아하지 않아. 너는 어때?)

   G: I like them a lot. (나는 거북이를 많이 좋아해.)

  3 **G:** Look at the lizards! (도마뱀 좀 봐!)

   B: Do you like them? (너는 도마뱀을 좋아하니?)

   G: Yes, I like lizards a lot.

    (응, 나는 도마뱀을 많이 좋아해.)

   B: Do you have a lizard? (너는 도마뱀을 기르니?)

   G: No, my mom doesn't like them.

    (아니, 엄마가 도마뱀을 좋아하지 않으셔.)

P.30~31 **UNIT TEST**

1 ⓐ rabbit (토끼)　　ⓑ fish (물고기)

  ⓒ cat (고양이)　　ⓓ turtle (거북이)

2 **B:** Do you like hamsters? (너는 햄스터를 좋아하니?)

  G: Yes, I do. How about you? (응, 좋아해. 너는 어때?)

  B: I like them, too. (나도 햄스터를 좋아해.)

3 **G:** Do you have any pets? (너는 애완동물을 기르니?)

  B: Yes, I have a dog and a rabbit.

    (응, 나는 개 한 마리와 토끼 한 마리를 길러.)

  Question: What does the boy have?

      (소년은 무엇을 기르는가?)

4 **W:** Do you like fish? (너는 물고기를 좋아하니?)

  ⓐ Yes, I like birds. (응, 나는 새를 좋아해.)

  ⓑ Yes, I do. (응, 좋아해.)

  ⓒ No, I don't have fish.

    (아니, 나는 물고기를 기르지 않아.)

  ⓓ How about you? (너는 어때?)

5 ⓐ **G:** I like turtles. How about you?

    (나는 거북이를 좋아해. 너는 어때?)

   B: I like them, too. (나도 거북이를 좋아해.)

  ⓑ **G:** Do you have any pets?

    (너는 애완동물을 기르니?)

   B: Yes, I have two turtles.

    (응, 나는 거북이 두 마리를 길러.)

  ⓒ **G:** Do you like hamsters?

    (너는 햄스터를 좋아하니?)

   B: Yes, I like them a lot.

    (응, 나는 햄스터를 많이 좋아해.)

11

ⓓ **G**: Do you have a rabbit? (너는 토끼를 기르니?)
　　B: No, I don't have a bird.
　　　　(아니, 나는 새를 기르지 않아.)

6　**B**: Look! What a cute bird!
　　　　(저것 봐! 정말 귀여운 새구나!)
　　G: Do you like birds? (너는 새를 좋아하니?)
　　B: Yes, I do. (응, 좋아해.)
　　G: Do you have a bird? (너는 새를 기르니?)
　　B: No, I don't. I have a lizard.
　　　　(아니, 기르지 않아. 나는 도마뱀 한 마리를 길러.)

　　Question: What is the boy's pet?
　　　　　　　(소년의 애완동물은 무엇인가?)

7　**G**: Do you have any pets? (너는 애완동물을 기르니?)
　　B: Yes, I have a cat. Do you like cats?
　　　　(응, 나는 고양이 한 마리를 길러. 너는 고양이를 좋아하니?)
　　G: No, I don't. But I like rabbits.
　　　　(아니, 좋아하지 않아. 하지만 나는 토끼를 좋아해.)
　　B: Oh, I like them, too. (오, 나도 토끼를 좋아해.)

　　Question: What does the girl like?
　　　　　　　(소녀는 무엇을 좋아하는가?)

P.32~33
REVIEW TEST 1　UNITS 1~3

| 1 ⓓ | 2 ⓒ | 3 ⓐ | 4 ⓓ | 5 ⓐ |
| 6 ⓓ | 7 ⓒ | 8 ⓒ | 9 ⓑ | 10 ⓒ |

1　ⓐ friend (친구)　　ⓑ nice (좋은, 즐거운)
　　ⓒ meet (만나다)　　ⓓ name (이름)

2　ⓐ rabbit (토끼)　　ⓑ fish (물고기)
　　ⓒ hamster (햄스터)　　ⓓ lizard (도마뱀)

3　**G**: Who is she? (그녀는 누구니?)
　　B: She is my baby sister. (그녀는 내 아기 여동생이야.)
　　G: What a cute girl! (정말 귀여운 소녀구나!)

4　**W**: Good morning, Alice. How are you today?
　　　　(안녕, Alice. 오늘 기분 어떠니?)
　　G: I'm good, thank you. And you?
　　　　(전 좋아요. 고맙습니다. 당신은요?)
　　W: ＿＿＿＿＿＿＿＿＿＿＿＿＿＿
　　ⓐ I'm glad to meet you. (만나서 반가워.)
　　ⓑ My name is Lisa. (내 이름은 Lisa란다.)
　　ⓒ This is my friend. (이분은 내 친구란다.)
　　ⓓ I'm good, too. Thanks. (나도 좋아. 고마워.)

5　**B**: What a cute turtle! (정말 귀여운 거북이구나!)
　　G: Do you like turtles? (너는 거북이를 좋아하니?)
　　B: ＿＿＿＿＿＿＿＿＿＿＿＿＿
　　ⓐ Yes, I do. (응, 좋아해.)
　　ⓑ No, they don't. (아니, 그들은 좋아하지 않아.)
　　ⓒ I have two turtles. (나는 거북이 두 마리를 길러.)
　　ⓓ I don't have any pets.
　　　　(나는 애완동물을 기르지 않아.)

6　ⓐ **B**: Who is he? (그는 누구니?)
　　　G: He is my father. (그는 우리 아빠야.)
　　ⓑ **B**: Do you have any pets?
　　　　　(너는 애완동물을 기르니?)
　　　G: No, I don't. (아니, 기르지 않아.)
　　ⓒ **B**: How old are you? (너는 몇 살이니?)
　　　G: I'm nine years old. (나는 아홉 살이야.)
　　ⓓ **B**: What's her name? (그녀의 이름은 뭐니?)
　　　G: She is my aunt. (그녀는 우리 이모야.)

7　ⓐ **G**: Good afternoon. How are you today?
　　　　　(안녕. 오늘 기분 어때?)
　　　B: I'm good. Thanks. (난 좋아. 고마워.)
　　ⓑ **G**: Do you have fish? (너는 물고기를 기르니?)
　　　B: Yes, I do. (응, 길러.)
　　ⓒ **G**: Do you have any brothers or sisters?
　　　　　(너는 형제나 자매가 있니?)
　　　B: No, they are friends. (아니, 그들은 친구야.)
　　ⓓ **G**: Nice to meet you. (만나서 반가워.)
　　　B: Nice to meet you, too. (나도 만나서 반가워.)

8　**G**: Do you have any pets? (너는 애완동물을 기르니?)
　　B: Yes, I have a cat and a bird. How about you?
　　　　(응, 나는 고양이 한 마리와 새 한 마리를 길러. 너는 어때?)
　　G: I have a dog. (나는 개 한 마리를 길러.)
　　B: Oh, I like dogs. (오, 나는 개를 좋아해.)

　　Question: Which one is the girl's pet?
　　　　　　　(소녀의 애완동물은 어느 것인가?)

9　**B**: Good morning, Lisa! (안녕, Lisa!)
　　G: Good morning! This is my brother.
　　　　(안녕! 얘는 내 남동생이야.)
　　B: What's his name? (그의 이름은 뭐니?)
　　G: His name is Joe. (그의 이름은 Joe야.)
　　B: Glad to meet you. (만나서 반가워.)

　　Question: Who is Joe? (Joe는 누구인가?)

10　**G**: Who are they? (그들은 누구니?)
　　 B: They are my twin sisters.
　　　　 (그들은 내 쌍둥이 여동생들이야.)
　　 G: How old are they? (그들은 몇 살이니?)

B: They are six years old. (그들은 여섯 살이야.)

G: Wow. They're so cute! (와. 정말 귀엽다!)

Question: How old are the boy's sisters?
(소년의 여동생들은 몇 살인가?)

UNIT 4 ART CLASS

ANSWERS

P.34

P.35

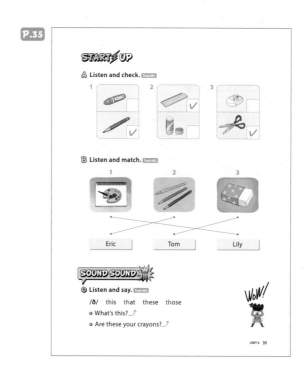

P.38~39 **DICTATION**

A
1 s 2 u, e 3 r, l
4 s, s 5 o, r, e

B
1 this 2 crayons 3 these
4 sketchbook 5 those

C
1 that, it
2 What, erasers
3 ruler, John's, glue, mine

P.40~41 **UNIT TEST**

1 ⓒ 2 ⓑ 3 ⓐ 4 ⓑ
5 ⓒ 6 ⓑ 7 ⓓ

SCRIPTS & 해석

P.34 **ARE YOU READY?**

⚡ **Listen and number.**
1 **W**: What's this? (이것은 무엇이니?)
　B: It's a cat. (그것은 고양이예요.)

2 **G**: Are these your crayons?
　　(이것들은 네 크레용이니?)
　B: No, they aren't. They are Emma's.
　　(아니, 그렇지 않아. 그것들은 Emma 거야.)

3 **G**: Is that your glue? (저것은 네 풀이니?)
　B: Oh, yes. It's mine. (오, 맞아. 그것은 내 거야.)

⭐ **Listen and repeat.**
crayon (크레용)　colored pencil (색연필)
eraser (지우개)　sketchbook (스케치북)
glue (풀)　scissors (가위)
ruler (자)

P.35 **START UP**

A **Listen and check.**
1 colored pencil (색연필)
2 ruler (자)
3 scissors (가위)

B **Listen and match.**
1 **G**: Is that Lily's sketchbook?
　　(저것은 Lily의 스케치북이니?)
　B: Yes, it is. (응, 그래.)

2 **B**: Are these Tom's colored pencils?
　　(이것들은 Tom의 색연필이니?)
　G: No, they aren't. They are Eric's.
　　(아니, 그렇지 않아. 그것들은 Eric 거야.)

3 **G**: Tom, what's that? (Tom, 저것은 무엇이니?)
　B: Oh, it's my eraser. (오, 그것은 내 지우개야.)

P.35 **SOUND SOUND**

🔊 **Listen and say.**

/ð/ this (이것)　　　that (저것)

　　these (이것들)　　those (저것들)

○ What's this? (이것은 무엇이니?)

○ Are these your crayons? (이것들은 네 크레용이니?)

P.36~37 **LISTEN UP**

🅐 **Listen and number.**

1　B: What's this? (이것은 무엇이니?)
　　G: It's Julie's glue. (그것은 Julie의 풀이야.)

2　G: What are those? (저것들은 무엇이니?)
　　B: They are crayons. They are Mike's.
　　　(그것들은 크레용이야. 그것들은 Mike 거야.)

3　B: What are these? (이것들은 무엇이니?)
　　G: They are Ann's rulers. (그것들은 Ann의 자야.)

🅑 **Listen and check.**

1　B: Is that your sketchbook?
　　　(저것은 네 스케치북이니?)
　　G: Yes, it is. (응, 그래.)
　　B: I have the same one.
　　　(나도 같은 스케치북이 있어.)

2　B: What's this? (이것은 무엇이니?)
　　G: It's my dream house. (그것은 내 꿈의 집이야.)
　　B: It looks nice. (멋져 보인다.)

3　G: Are these your crayons?
　　　(이것들은 네 크레용이니?)
　　B: Yes, they are. (응, 그래.)
　　G: Here you are. (여기 있어.)

4　B: What are those? (저것들은 무엇이니?)
　　G: They are my erasers. (그것들은 내 지우개야.)
　　B: Wow, you have a lot. (와, 너 많이 가지고 있구나.)

🅒 **Listen and check.**

1　B: Kate, is this your ruler? (Kate, 이것은 네 자니?)
　　G: No, it isn't. It's John's.
　　　(아니, 그렇지 않아. 그것은 John 거야.)
　　B: Oh, I see. Is that your sketchbook?
　　　(오, 그렇구나. 저것은 네 스케치북이니?)
　　G: Yes, it's mine. (응, 그것은 내 거야.)

　　Question: The sketchbook is Kate's.
　　　　　　(스케치북은 Kate의 것이다.)

2　G: What are those? (저것들은 무엇이니?)
　　B: They are scissors. (그것들은 가위야.)
　　G: Are they yours? (그것들은 네 거니?)
　　B: No, they are Amy's. (아니, 그것들은 Amy 거야.)

　　Question: They are the boy's scissors.
　　　　　　(그것들은 소년의 가위이다.)

🅓 **Listen and write.**

1　B: What's this? (이것은 무엇이니?)
　　G: It's my cat, Leo. (그것은 내 고양이 Leo야.)
　　B: You did a good job. (잘 만들었구나.)

2　G: Are these tigers? (이것들은 호랑이니?)
　　B: No, they are lions. (아니, 그것들은 사자야.)
　　G: Oh, I see. They are a family of lions.
　　　(오, 그렇구나. 그것들은 사자 가족이구나.)

3　B: What are those? (저것들은 무엇이니?)
　　G: They are rabbits. (그것들은 토끼야.)
　　B: How cute! (귀엽다!)

4　G: Is that a dog? (저것은 개니?)
　　B: Yes, it is. It's my dog, Toto.
　　　(응, 그래. 그것은 내 개 Toto야.)
　　G: What a nice picture! (정말 멋진 그림이구나!)

P.37 **LET'S SPEAK WITH BUDDY**

🔊 **Listen and say.**

Jenny: What's that? (그것은 무엇이니?)
Jack: It's a tiger. (그것은 호랑이야.)
Jenny: Wow, cool! (와, 멋지다!)

Jenny: Is that your picture? (그것은 네 그림이니?)
Jack: Umm… (음…)
Ann: No!! That's mine! (아니!! 그것은 내 거야!)

P.38~39 **DICTATION**

🅐　1　eraser (지우개)
　　2　glue (풀)
　　3　ruler (자)
　　4　scissors (가위)
　　5　colored pencil (색연필)

🅑　1　What's this? (이것은 무엇이니?)
　　2　They are my crayons. (그것들은 내 크레용이야.)
　　3　Are these tigers? (이것들은 호랑이니?)
　　4　Is that your sketchbook?
　　　　(저것은 네 스케치북이니?)

15

5 What are those? (저것들은 무엇이니?)

C 1 B: Is that your sketchbook?
(저것은 네 스케치북이니?)
G: Yes, it is. (응, 그래.)
B: I have the same one.
(나도 같은 스케치북이 있어.)

2 B: What are those? (저것들은 무엇이니?)
G: They are my erasers. (그것들은 내 지우개야.)
B: Wow, you have a lot. (와, 너 많이 가지고 있구나.)

3 B: Kate, is this your ruler? (Kate, 이것은 네 자니?)
G: No, it isn't. It's John's.
(아니, 그렇지 않아. 그것은 John 거야.)
B: Oh, I see. Is that your glue?
(오, 그렇구나. 저것은 네 풀이니?)
G: Yes, it's mine. (응, 그것은 내 거야.)

P.40~41 UNIT TEST

1 ⓐ crayon (크레용)   ⓑ glue (풀)
ⓒ scissors (가위)   ⓓ ruler (자)

2 ⓐ This is my sketchbook. (이것은 내 스케치북이다.)
ⓑ That is my sketchbook. (저것은 내 스케치북이다.)
ⓒ These are my sketchbooks.
(이것들은 내 스케치북들이다.)
ⓓ Those are my sketchbooks.
(저것들은 내 스케치북들이다.)

3 B: Is this your ruler? (이것은 네 자니?)
G: Yes, it is. (응, 그래.)
B: Here you are. (여기 있어.)

4 W: Are these your crayons? (이것들은 네 크레용이니?)
ⓐ No, they are my crayons.
(아니, 그것들은 내 크레용이야.)
ⓑ Yes, they are mine. (응, 그것들은 내 거야.)
ⓒ No, it's Mike's. (아니, 그것은 Mike 거야.)
ⓓ Yes, they are crayons. (응, 그것들은 크레용이야.)

5 ⓐ G: What are these? (이것들은 무엇이니?)
B: They are Peter's scissors.
(그것들은 Peter의 가위야.)
ⓑ G: Are those your erasers?
(저것들은 네 지우개니?)
B: No, they aren't. (아니, 그렇지 않아.)
ⓒ G: Is this your ruler? (이것은 네 자니?)
B: Yes, they are. (응, 그래.)
ⓓ G: What's that? (저것은 무엇이니?)
B: Oh, it's my pencil. (오, 그것은 내 연필이야.)

6 G: Tony, is that your picture?
(Tony, 저것은 네 그림이니?)
B: Yes, it is. (응, 그래)
G: I like your picture. What are those?
(네 그림이 맘에 들어. 저것들은 무엇이니?)
B: They are tigers. (그것들은 호랑이야.)

Question: Which one is the boy's picture?
(어느 것이 소년의 그림인가?)

7 G: James, is this your crayon?
(James, 이것은 네 크레용이니?)
B: No, it's not. It's Tom's.
(아니, 그렇지 않아. 그것은 Tom 거야.)
G: Are these your colored pencils?
(이것들은 네 색연필이니?)
B: Yes, they are. (응, 그래.)
G: Here you are. (여기 있어.)

Question: James has colored pencils.
(James는 색연필들을 가지고 있다.)

UNIT 5 MUSIC

ANSWERS

P.42

P.43

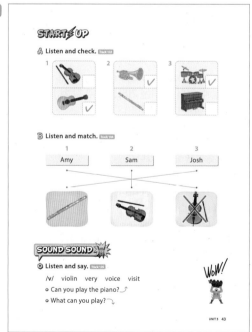

P.44

P.45

P.46~47 DICTATION

A 1 c   2 l, u   3 p, i
   4 v, i   5 u, i

B 1 play   2 trumpet   3 can't
   4 can   5 drums

C 1 guitar, can
2 What, trumpet
3 piano, violin, play

P.48~49 **UNIT TEST**

1 ⓓ 2 ⓑ 3 ⓐ 4 ⓒ
5 ⓑ 6 ⓐ 7 ⓓ

SCRIPTS & 해석

P.42 **ARE YOU READY?**

⚡ **Listen and number.**

1 **G**: Can you play the piano?
(너는 피아노를 칠 수 있니?)
B: Yes, I can. (응, 칠 수 있어.)

2 **M**: Can you play the drums?
(너는 드럼을 칠 수 있니?)
G: No, I can't. (아뇨, 못 쳐요.)

3 **G**: What can you play?
(너는 무엇을 연주할 수 있니?)
B: I can play the cello. (난 첼로를 켤 수 있어.)

⭐ **Listen and repeat.**

piano (피아노)   violin (바이올린)   cello (첼로)
flute (플루트)   guitar (기타)   drums (드럼)
trumpet (트럼펫)

P.43 **START UP**

Ⓐ **Listen and check.**

1 guitar (기타)
2 trumpet (트럼펫)
3 drums (드럼)

Ⓑ **Listen and match.**

1 **B**: Amy, can you play the cello?
(Amy, 너는 첼로를 켤 수 있니?)
G: No, I can't. (아니, 못 켜.)

2 **W**: Sam, what can you play?
(Sam, 너는 무엇을 연주할 수 있니?)
B: I can play the violin.
(저는 바이올린을 켤 수 있어요.)

3 **G**: Can Josh play the flute?

(Josh는 플루트를 불 수 있니?)
B: Yes, he can. (응, 불 수 있어.)

P.43 **SOUND SOUND**

🔊 **Listen and say.**

/v/ violin (바이올린)   very (매우, 아주)
voice (목소리)   visit (방문하다)
◦ Can you play the piano? (너는 피아노를 칠 수 있니?)
◦ What can you play? (너는 무엇을 연주할 수 있니?)

P.44~45 **LISTEN UP**

Ⓐ **Listen and circle.**

1 **B**: Can you play the flute?
(너는 플루트를 불 수 있니?)
G: Yes, I can. (응, 불 수 있어.)

2 **B**: Can he play the piano?
(그는 피아노를 칠 수 있니?)
G: No, he can't. He's terrible.
(아니, 못 쳐. 그는 형편없어.)

3 **B**: Can she play the cello?
(그녀는 첼로를 켤 수 있니?)
G: Yes, she plays it very well.
(응, 그녀는 첼로를 아주 잘 켜.)

Ⓑ **Listen and check.**

1 **B**: Can she play the guitar?
(그녀는 기타를 칠 수 있니?)
G: Yes, she can. She plays it very well.
(응, 칠 수 있어. 그녀는 기타를 아주 잘 쳐.)
B: Wow, cool! (와, 멋지다!)

2 **G**: Can you play the cello?
(너는 첼로를 켤 수 있니?)
B: No, I can't. But I can play the violin.
(아니, 못 켜. 하지만 난 바이올린을 켤 수 있어.)
G: Nice! (멋지다!)

3 **G**: Can your brother play the drums?
(너희 형은 드럼을 칠 수 있니?)
B: No, he can't. He's not good at music.
(아니, 못 쳐. 그는 음악을 잘하지 못해.)

4 **B**: What can they play?
(그들은 무엇을 연주할 수 있니?)
G: They can play the trumpet.
(그들은 트럼펫을 불 수 있어.)

B: Great! (멋지다!)

C **Listen and check.**

1 **B**: Can James play the cello?
(James는 첼로를 켤 수 있니?)
G: Yes, he plays it very well.
(응, 그는 첼로를 아주 잘 켜.)
B: Wow, good! What can you play?
(와, 대단하다! 너는 무엇을 연주할 수 있니?)
G: I can play the drums. (나는 드럼을 칠 수 있어.)
B: Cool! (멋지다!)

Question: The girl can play the drums.
(소녀는 드럼을 칠 수 있다.)

2 **B**: Can you play the piano?
(너는 피아노를 칠 수 있니?)
G: Yes, I can. How about you?
(응, 칠 수 있어. 너는 어때?)
B: I can't play the piano, but I can play the violin.
(나는 피아노를 못 치지만, 바이올린을 켤 수 있어.)
G: Nice! We can play together.
(멋지다! 우리는 함께 연주할 수 있어.)
B: Great. (좋아.)

Question: The boy can play the piano and the violin.
(소년은 피아노와 바이올린을 연주할 수 있다.)

D **Listen and mark.**

B: My family loves music, and we play together.
(우리 가족은 음악을 대단히 좋아하고, 우리는 함께 연주를 해.)
G: Wow, great! What can you play?
(와, 멋지다! 너는 무엇을 연주할 수 있니?)
B: I can play the flute. (나는 플루트를 불 수 있어.)
G: How about your father? (너희 아빠는?)
B: He can play the trumpet.
(그는 트럼펫을 부실 수 있어.)
G: Can your mother play the piano?
(너희 엄마는 피아노를 치실 수 있니?)
B: No, she can't. But she can play the guitar and the violin.
(아니, 못 치셔. 하지만 그녀는 기타와 바이올린을 연주하실 수 있어.)

P.45 **LET'S SPEAK WITH BUDDY**

Listen and say.

M1: Can you play the violin?
(너는 바이올린을 켤 수 있니?)
Jack: No, I can't. (아뇨, 못 켜요.)

W: Can you play the cello? (너는 첼로를 켤 수 있니?)
Jack: No, I can't. (아뇨, 못 켜요.)

M2: What can you play? (너는 무엇을 연주할 수 있니?)

Jack: I can play the triangle.
(저는 트라이앵글을 칠 수 있어요.)

P.46~47 **DICTATION**

A 1 cello (첼로)
2 flute (플루트)
3 piano (피아노)
4 violin (바이올린)
5 guitar (기타)

B 1 She can play the cello. (그녀는 첼로를 켤 수 있어.)
2 Can you play the trumpet?
(너는 트럼펫을 불 수 있니?)
3 I can't play the guitar. (나는 기타를 못 쳐.)
4 What can you play? (너는 무엇을 연주할 수 있니?)
5 He plays the drums very well.
(그는 드럼을 아주 잘 쳐.)

C 1 **B**: Can she play the guitar?
(그녀는 기타를 칠 수 있니?)
G: Yes, she can. She plays it very well.
(응, 칠 수 있어. 그녀는 기타를 아주 잘 쳐.)
B: Wow, cool! (와, 멋지다!)

2 **B**: What can they play?
(그들은 무엇을 연주할 수 있니?)
G: They can play the trumpet.
(그들은 트럼펫을 불 수 있어.)
B: Great! (멋지다!)

3 **B**: Can you play the piano?
(너는 피아노를 칠 수 있니?)
G: Yes, I can. How about you?
(응, 칠 수 있어. 너는 어때?)
B: I can't play the piano, but I can play the violin.
(나는 피아노를 못 치지만, 바이올린을 켤 수 있어.)
G: Nice! We can play together.
(멋지다! 우리는 함께 연주할 수 있어.)

B: Great. (좋아.)

1 ⓐ guitar (기타)   ⓑ flute (플루트)
   ⓒ drums (드럼)   ⓓ trumpet (트럼펫)

2 ⓐ He can play the guitar. (그는 기타를 칠 수 있다.)
   ⓑ He can't play the drums. (그는 드럼을 못 친다.)
   ⓒ She can play the drums. (그녀는 드럼을 칠 수 있다.)
   ⓓ She can't play the guitar. (그녀는 기타를 못 친다.)

3 **B**: Can he play the flute? (그는 플루트를 불 수 있니?)
   G: Yes, he plays it very well.
      (응, 그는 플루트를 아주 잘 불어.)
   B: Great! (멋지다!)

4 **B**: What can she play? (그녀는 무엇을 연주할 수 있니?)
   ⓐ I can play the piano. (나는 피아노를 칠 수 있어.)
   ⓑ Yes, she plays it very well.
      (응, 그녀는 그것을 아주 잘 연주해.)
   ⓒ She can play the guitar. (그녀는 기타를 칠 수 있어.)
   ⓓ No, she's not good at music.
      (아니, 그녀는 음악을 잘하지 못해.)

5 ⓐ **G**: Can you play the violin?
         (너는 바이올린을 켤 수 있니?)
      B: No, I can't. (아니, 못 켜.)
   ⓑ **G**: Can he play the flute?
         (그는 플루트를 불 수 있니?)
      B: Yes, he can play the trumpet.
         (응, 그는 트럼펫을 불 수 있어.)
   ⓒ **G**: What can you play?
         (너는 무엇을 연주할 수 있니?)
      B: I can play the triangle.
         (나는 트라이앵글을 칠 수 있어.)
   ⓓ **G**: Can they play the drums?
         (그들은 드럼을 칠 수 있니?)
      B: Yes, they play them very well.
         (응, 그들은 드럼을 아주 잘 쳐.)

6 **B**: Can you play the piano?
      (너는 피아노를 칠 수 있니?)
   G: No, but I can play the drums.
      (아니, 하지만 난 드럼을 칠 수 있어.)
   B: Nice! (멋지다!)

   Question: What can't the girl play?
            (소녀가 연주할 수 없는 것은 무엇인가?)

7 **G**: Can you play the violin?
      (너는 바이올린을 켤 수 있니?)

B: Yes, I can. What can you play?
   (응, 켤 수 있어. 너는 무엇을 연주할 수 있니?)
G: I can play the cello. (나는 첼로를 켤 수 있어.)
B: Wow, cool! We can play together!
   (와, 멋지다! 우리는 함께 연주할 수 있어!)
Question: They can play the violin and the cello.
         (그들은 바이올린과 첼로를 연주할 수 있다.)

UNIT 6 YUMMY FOOD

ANSWERS

P.50

UNIT 6
YUMMY FOOD

ARE YOU READY?

Listen and number.

Listen and repeat.

bread   sandwich   salad   pizza

chicken   noodles   fried rice

50

P.51

START UP

A Listen and number.

2   4   1   3

B Listen and match.

1	2	3
Ben	Sarah	Peter

salad	bread	chicken

SOUND SOUND

Listen and say.

/p/ pizza picture park   /b/ bread breakfast big

Listen and circle.

1 /p/ (/b/)   2 (/p/) /b/   3 /p/ (/b/)

UNIT 6   51

P.52

LISTEN UP

A Listen and circle.

B Listen and check.

C Listen and check.

	TRUE	FALSE
1 The boy wants some pizza.	✓	
2 The girl doesn't want ice cream.		✓

52

P.53

D Listen and write.

1 I want ...   (b) (e)

2 I want ...   (c) (d)

LET'S SPEAK WITH BUDDY

Listen and say.

What do you want?   I want some chicken.   Do you want some salad?   Yes, I do.

Do you want some pizza?   Yes, please.   How about noodles?   No, thank you. I'm full.

With these words, role-play with your buddy!

bread	sandwiches	fried rice	fruit	ice cream

UNIT 6   53

P.54~55 **DICTATION**

A 1 a   2 p, i   3 c, k
    4 e, a   5 o, o

B 1 want   2 fruit   3 about
    4 full   5 sandwich

C 1 pizza, thank
  2 want, chicken
  3 bread, No, fried, rice, salad

UNIT TEST

1 ⓒ   2 ⓒ   3 ⓑ   4 ⓓ
5 ⓐ   6 ⓑ   7 ⓒ

SCRIPTS & 해석

P.50 ARE YOU READY?

⚡ Listen and number.

1 W: Do you want some pizza? (피자 좀 먹을래?)
  B: Yes, please. Thank you. (네, 주세요. 고맙습니다.)

2 G: What do you want? (너 뭐 먹을래?)
  B: I want chicken. (닭고기 먹고 싶어.)

3 B: Do you want a sandwich? (샌드위치 먹을래?)
  G: No, thanks. (아니, 괜찮아.)

⭐ Listen and repeat.

bread (빵)   sandwich (샌드위치)
salad (샐러드)   pizza (피자)
chicken (닭고기)   noodles (국수)
fried rice (볶음밥)

P.51 START UP

A Listen and number.

1 fried rice (볶음밥)
2 noodles (국수)
3 sandwich (샌드위치)
4 pizza (피자)

B Listen and match.

1 W: Ben, what do you want?
    (Ben, 너 뭐 먹을래?)
  B: Chicken, please. (닭고기 주세요.)

2 W: Sarah, do you want some bread?
    (Sarah, 빵 좀 먹을래?)
  G: Yes, thank you. (네, 고맙습니다.)

3 W: Peter, what do you want?
    (Peter, 너 뭐 먹을래?)
  B: I want some salad. (샐러드 좀 먹고 싶어요.)

P.51 SOUND SOUND

🔊 Listen and say.

/p/ pizza (피자)   picture (그림, 사진)   park (공원)
/b/ bread (빵)   breakfast (아침 식사)   big (큰)

✚ Listen and circle.

1 big   2 picture   3 breakfast

P.52~53 LISTEN UP

A Listen and circle.

1 B: Do you want some bread? (빵 좀 먹을래?)
  G: Yes, please. I like bread. (응, 줘. 난 빵 좋아해.)

2 B: Do you want some chicken?
    (닭고기 좀 먹을래?)
  G: No, I don't like chicken.
    (아니, 난 닭고기를 좋아하지 않아.)

3 M: Do you want some noodles? (국수 좀 먹을래?)
  B: No, thank you. I'm full.
    (아뇨, 괜찮아요. 배불러요.)

B Listen and check.

1 G: Do you want some salad? (샐러드 좀 먹을래?)
  B: Yes, thank you. (응, 고마워.)
  G: Help yourself. (많이 먹어.)

2 B: Do you want a sandwich? (샌드위치 먹을래?)
  G: No, I don't. (아니, 안 먹을래.)
  B: Then, how about some pizza?
    (그럼, 피자는 어때?)

3 W: Do you want some more? (더 먹을래?)
  B: No, thank you. I'm full.
    (아뇨, 괜찮아요. 배불러요.)
  W: Okay. (알겠어.)

4 B: What do you want? (너 뭐 먹을래?)
  G: Do you have some fruit? (과일 있니?)
  B: Yes, I do. Here you are. (응, 있어. 여기 있어.)

C Listen and check.

1 B: I'm hungry. (저 배고파요.)
  W: What do you want? (뭐 먹을래?)
  B: Do you have pizza? (피자 있어요?)
  W: Yes, I do. Here you are.
    (그래, 있단다. 여기 있다.)

  Question: The boy wants some pizza.
    (소년은 피자를 원한다.)

2 B: Do you want some noodles? (국수 좀 먹을래?)
G: No, I don't. (아니, 안 먹을래.)
B: Then, how about ice cream?
(그럼, 아이스크림은 어때?)
G: Yes, please. (응, 줘.)

Question: The girl doesn't want ice cream.
(소녀는 아이스크림을 원하지 않는다.)

Ⓓ **Listen and write.**

1 W: Dan, what do you want? (Dan, 뭐 먹을래?)
B: Do you have pizza and chicken?
(피자와 닭고기 있어요?)
W: Yes, I do. Here you are. Help yourself.
(그래, 있단다. 여기 있다. 많이 먹으렴.)

2 W: Sue, do you want some bread?
(Sue, 빵 좀 먹을래?)
G: No, thank you. (아뇨, 괜찮아요.)
W: Then, how about some fried rice?
(그럼, 볶음밥은 어떠니?)
G: Oh, thank you. Do you have some salad,
too? (오, 고맙습니다. 샐러드도 있나요?)
W: Yes, I do. Help yourself.
(그래, 있단다. 많이 먹으렴.)

Ⓑ **1** What do you want? (너 뭐 먹을래?)
2 Do you have some fruit? (과일 있니?)
3 How about some ice cream? (아이스크림은 어때?)
4 No, thank you. I'm full. (아뇨, 괜찮아요. 배불러요.)
5 Do you want a sandwich? (샌드위치 먹을래?)

Ⓒ **1** G: Do you want some pizza? (피자 좀 먹을래?)
B: Yes, thank you. (응, 고마워.)
G: Help yourself. (많이 먹어.)

2 W: Dan, what do you want? (Dan, 뭐 먹을래?)
B: Do you have pizza and chicken?
(피자와 닭고기 있어요?)
W: Yes, I do. Here you are.
(그래, 있단다. 여기 있다.)

3 W: Sue, do you want some bread?
(Sue, 빵 좀 먹을래?)
G: No, thank you. (아뇨, 괜찮아요.)
W: Then, how about some fried rice?
(그럼, 볶음밥은 어떠니?)
G: Oh, thank you. Do you have some salad,
too? (오, 고맙습니다. 샐러드도 있나요?)
W: Yes, I do. Help yourself.
(그래, 있단다. 많이 먹으렴.)

P.53 **LET'S SPEAK WITH BUDDY**

🔘 **Listen and say.**

Jenny: What do you want? (너 뭐 먹을래?)
Jack: I want some chicken. (닭고기 먹고 싶어.)

Jenny: Do you want some salad?
(샐러드 좀 먹을래?)
Jack: Yes, I do. (응, 먹을래.)

Jenny: Do you want some pizza? (피자 좀 먹을래?)
Jack: Yes, please. (응, 줘.)

Jenny: How about noodles? (국수는 어때?)
Jack: No, thank you. I'm full.
(아니, 괜찮아. 배불러.)

P.54~55 **DICTATION**

Ⓐ **1** salad (샐러드)
2 pizza (피자)
3 chicken (닭고기)
4 bread (빵)
5 noodles (국수)

P.56~57 **UNIT TEST**

1 ⓐ salad (샐러드) ⓑ fried rice (볶음밥)
ⓒ bread (빵) ⓓ chicken (닭고기)

2 ⓐ She wants some pizza and fruit.
(그녀는 피자와 과일을 원한다.)
ⓑ She doesn't want any chicken or salad.
(그녀는 닭고기나 샐러드를 원하지 않는다.)
ⓒ She wants some pizza and chicken.
(그녀는 피자와 닭고기를 원한다.)
ⓓ She doesn't want any pizza or chicken.
(그녀는 피자나 닭고기를 원하지 않는다.)

3 B: Do you want some more? (더 먹을래?)
G: No, thanks. I'm full. (아니, 괜찮아. 배불러.)
B: Okay. (알겠어.)

4 G: What do you want? (너 뭐 먹을래?)
B: Do you have some sandwiches? (샌드위치 있니?)
G: _____
ⓐ I like salad. (난 샐러드 좋아해.)
ⓑ No, thanks. I'm full. (아니, 괜찮아. 배불러.)
ⓒ Yes, please. (응, 줘.)
ⓓ Yes. Here you are. (응. 여기 있어.)

23

5 ⓐ **G**: Do you want some pizza? (피자 좀 먹을래?)
    B: Help yourself. (많이 먹어.)
  ⓑ **G**: What do you want? (너 뭐 먹을래?)
    B: Chicken, please. (닭고기 줘.)
  ⓒ **G**: Do you want some more? (더 먹을래?)
    B: No, thank you. I'm full. (아니, 괜찮아. 배불러.)
  ⓓ **G**: Do you have some fried rice? (볶음밥 있니?)
    B: Yes. Here you are. (응. 여기 있어.)

6 **W**: Do you want some pizza? (피자 좀 먹을래?)
 B: No, I don't. (아뇨, 안 먹을래요.)
 W: Then, how about chicken?
   (그럼, 닭고기는 어떠니?)
 B: Yes, please. I like chicken.
   (네, 주세요. 전 닭고기 좋아해요.)
 W: Here you are. Help yourself.
   (여기 있다. 많이 먹으렴.)

 Question: What does the boy want?
     (소년은 무엇을 원하는가?)

7 **G**: What do you want? (너 뭐 먹을래?)
 B: Umm… Do you have some bread? (음… 빵 있니?)
 G: No, I don't. (아니, 없어.)
 B: How about some fried rice? (볶음밥은?)
 G: No. I have some salad and noodles. Do you
   want some? (없어. 샐러드와 국수가 있어. 좀 먹을래?)
 B: Yes, thank you. (그래, 고마워.)

 Question: What does the girl have?
     (소녀는 무엇을 가지고 있는가?)

P.58~59
REVIEW TEST 2 UNITS 4~6

| 1 ⓒ | 2 ⓑ | 3 ⓐ | 4 ⓑ | 5 ⓒ |
| 6 ⓓ | 7 ⓒ | 8 ⓓ | 9 ⓑ | 10 ⓓ |

1 ⓐ crayon (크레용)   ⓑ glue (풀)
  ⓒ ruler (자)   ⓓ eraser (지우개)

2 ⓐ violin (바이올린)   ⓑ guitar (기타)
  ⓒ flute (플루트)   ⓓ trumpet (트럼펫)

3 **B**: I'm hungry. (저 배고파요.)
 W: What do you want? (뭐 먹을래?)
 B: Do you have some fried rice? (볶음밥 있어요?)
 W: Yes, I do. Help yourself.
   (그래, 있단다. 많이 먹으렴.)

4 **G**: Is this your sketchbook? (이것은 네 스케치북이니?)

 B: No, it isn't. It's Peter's.
   (아니, 그렇지 않아. 그것은 Peter 거야.)
 G: Are these your crayons? (이것들은 네 크레용이니?)
 B: _____
 ⓐ No, it's Peter's. (아니, 그것은 Peter 거야.)
 ⓑ Yes, they're mine. (응, 그것들은 내 거야.)
 ⓒ It's not my crayon. (그것은 내 크레용이 아니야.)
 ⓓ They're colored pencils. (그것들은 색연필이야.)

5 **B**: Do you want some chicken? (치킨 좀 먹을래?)
 G: No, I don't. (아니, 안 먹을래.)
 B: How about some salad? (샐러드는 어때?)
 G: _____
 ⓐ Yes, here you are. (응, 여기 있어.)
 ⓑ Yes, I like sandwiches. (응, 나는 샌드위치를 좋아해.)
 ⓒ No, thanks. I'm full. (아니, 괜찮아. 배불러.)
 ⓓ No, I don't like chicken.
   (아니, 나는 닭고기를 좋아하지 않아.)

6 ⓐ **B**: Is that your picture? (저것은 네 그림이니?)
    G: Yes, it is. (응, 그래.)
  ⓑ **B**: Do you have pizza? (피자 있니?)
    G: No, I don't. (아니, 없어.)
  ⓒ **B**: Are those tigers? (저것들은 호랑이니?)
    G: No, they aren't. (아니, 그렇지 않아.)
  ⓓ **B**: Can they play the drums?
      (그들은 드럼을 칠 수 있니?)
    G: Yes, they are. (응, 그래.)

7 ⓐ **G**: What can you play?
      (너는 무엇을 연주할 수 있니?)
    B: I can play the guitar. (나는 기타를 칠 수 있어.)
  ⓑ **G**: What do you want? (너 뭐 먹을래?)
    B: I want some sandwiches. (샌드위치 먹고 싶어.)
  ⓒ **G**: What are these? (이것들은 무엇이니?)
    B: They are mine. (그것들은 내 거야.)
  ⓓ **G**: Can he play the flute?
      (그는 플루트를 불 수 있니?)
    B: Yes, he can. (응, 불 수 있어.)

8 **B**: Kate, can you play the piano?
   (Kate, 너는 피아노를 칠 수 있니?)
 G: No, I can't. (아니, 못 쳐.)
 B: How about the violin or the flute?
   (바이올린이나 플루트는 어때?)
 G: No, but I can play the cello.
   (못해, 하지만 나는 첼로를 켤 수 있어.)

 Question: Who is Kate? (누가 Kate인가?)

9 **B**: What are those? (저것들은 무엇이니?)
 G: They are Ben's colored pencils.

24

(그것들은 Ben의 색연필이야.)

B: Are these Ben's erasers?
(이것들은 Ben의 지우개니?)

G: No, they are mine. (아니, 그것들은 내 거야.)

B: Wow, you have a lot.
(와, 너 많이 가지고 있구나.)

Question: The girl has <u>erasers.</u>
(소녀는 <u>지우개들</u>을 가지고 있다.)

10 **W**: Do you want some bread? (빵 좀 먹을래?)

B: No, I don't. (아뇨, 안 먹을래요.)

W: How about some noodles? (국수는 어떠니?)

B: No, thank you. Do you have some fruit?
(아뇨, 괜찮아요. 과일 있나요?)

W: Yes, I do. Here you are. (그래, 있단다. 여기 있다.)

Question: The boy wants some <u>fruit.</u>
(소년은 <u>과일</u>을 원한다.)

ANSWERS

P.60

P.61

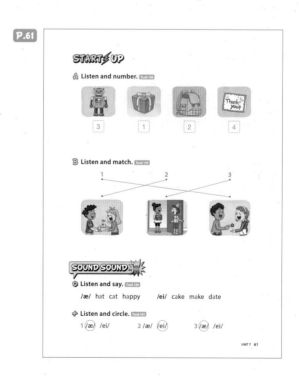

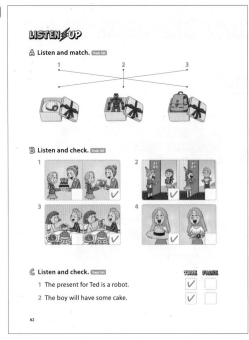

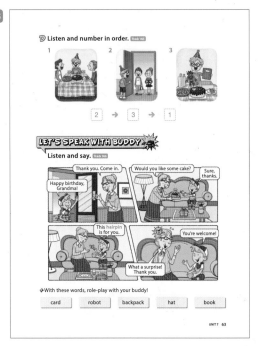

UNIT 7 63

P.64~65 DICTATION

A 1 a 2 a 3 e
4 a, i 5 c, k

B 1 birthday 2 robot 3 surprise
4 Thank 5 Would

C 1 Happy, card
2 hat, cake
3 present, robot, a, lot

P.66~67 UNIT TEST

1 ⓐ 2 ⓐ 3 ⓒ 4 ⓓ
5 ⓓ 6 ⓑ 7 ⓒ

SCRIPTS & 해석

P.60 ARE YOU READY?

⚡ **Listen and number.**

1 **G1**: Thank you for coming. (와줘서 고마워.)
B: My pleasure. (천만에.)

2 **B**: Happy birthday! This is for you.
(생일 축하해! 이건 네 거야.)
G1: Oh, thank you. (오, 고마워.)

3 **G1**: Would you like some cake?
(케이크 좀 먹을래?)
G2: Yes, please. Thanks. (응, 줘. 고마워.)

⭐ **Listen and repeat.**

card (카드) cake (케이크) present (선물)
hairpin (머리핀) robot (로봇) backpack (배낭)
hat (모자)

P.61 START UP

A **Listen and number.**

1 present (선물)
2 backpack (배낭)
3 robot (로봇)
4 card (카드)

B **Listen and match.**

1 **B**: This hairpin is for you. (이 머리핀은 네 거야.)
G: What a surprise! (놀랍구나!)

2 **B**: Would you like some cake? (케이크 좀 먹을래?)
G: Yes, thank you. (응, 고마워.)

3 **G**: Happy birthday! (생일 축하해!)
B: Thank you. Please come in. (고마워. 들어와.)

26

SOUND SOUND

🔊 **Listen and say.**

/æ/ hat (모자) cat (고양이) happy (행복한)

/ei/ cake (케이크) make (만들다) date (날짜)

➕ **Listen and circle.**

1 hat 2 make 3 cat

LISTEN UP

Ⓐ **Listen and match.**

1 W: This is for you. (이건 네 거란다.)
B: Oh, it's a backpack. Thanks a lot!
(오, 배낭이네요. 정말 감사합니다!)

2 G: I have a surprise present for you.
(널 위한 깜짝 선물이야.)
B: How nice of you! I like this robot.
(정말 친절하구나! 이 로봇 맘에 들어.)

3 M: This hat is for you. (이 모자는 당신 거예요.)
W: What a surprise! (놀랍군요!)

Ⓑ **Listen and check.**

1 G: Happy birthday, Grandma! This card is for you.
(생신 축하드려요, 할머니! 이 카드는 할머니 거예요.)
W: Oh, thank you. (오, 고맙구나.)
G: You're welcome. (천만에요.)

2 B: Thank you for coming. (와줘서 고마워.)
G: My pleasure. (천만에.)
B: Help yourself and have fun!
(많이 먹고 재미있게 놀아!)

3 B: Happy birthday! (생일 축하해!)
G: Thank you. Would you like some juice?
(고마워. 주스 좀 마실래?)
B: Sure. Thanks. (응. 고마워.)

4 B: Happy birthday, Mom! This is for you.
(생신 축하드려요, 엄마! 이건 엄마 거예요.)
W: Oh, I like this hat. Thank you.
(오, 이 모자 맘에 드는구나. 고마워.)
B: You're welcome. (천만에요.)

Ⓒ **Listen and check.**

1 G: Happy birthday, Ted! This present is for you. (생일 축하해, Ted! 이 선물은 네 거야.)
B: What a surprise! What is it?
(놀랍구나! 이거 뭐야?)

G: Open it. (열어봐.)
B: Oh, I like this robot. Thanks a lot.
(오, 이 로봇 맘에 들어. 정말 고마워.)
G: My pleasure. (천만에.)

Question: The present for Ted is a robot.
(Ted를 위한 선물은 로봇이다.)

2 B: Happy birthday! (생일 축하해!)
G: Thank you for coming to my party.
(파티에 와줘서 고마워.)
B: Sure. This card is for you.
(천만에. 이 카드는 네 거야.)
G: Oh, thank you. Would you like some cake?
(오, 고마워. 케이크 좀 먹을래?)
B: Yes, please. (응, 줘.)

Question: The boy will have some cake.
(소년은 케이크를 먹을 것이다.)

Ⓓ **Listen and number in order.**

G, B1: Happy birthday! (생일 축하해!)
B2: Thank you for coming. (와줘서 고마워.)
G, B1: This is for you. (이건 네 거야.)
B2: What a surprise! I love this robot and book. Thanks a lot.
(놀랍구나! 이 로봇과 책 맘에 들어. 정말 고마워.)
G, B1: You're welcome. (천만에.)
B2: Help yourselves and have a good time.
(많이 먹고 좋은 시간 보내.)

LET'S SPEAK WITH BUDDY

🔊 **Listen and say.**

Kevin: Happy birthday, Grandma!
(생신 축하드려요, 할머니!)
Grandma: Thank you. Come in. (고맙구나. 들어오렴.)

Grandma: Would you like some cake?
(케이크 좀 먹을래?)
Kevin: Sure, thanks. (네, 감사합니다.)

Kevin: This hairpin is for you.
(이 머리핀은 할머니 거예요.)

Grandma: What a surprise! Thank you.
(놀랍구나! 고맙다.)
Kevin: You're welcome! (천만에요!)

DICTATION

Ⓐ 1 hat (모자)

2 cake (케이크)

3 present (선물)

4 hairpin (머리핀)

5 backpack (배낭)

Ⓑ **1** Happy birthday! (생일 축하해!)

2 This robot is for you. (이 로봇은 네 거야.)

3 What a surprise! (놀랍구나!)

4 Thank you for coming. (와줘서 고마워.)

5 Would you like some cake? (케이크 좀 먹을래?)

Ⓒ **1** G: Happy birthday, Grandma! This card is for you.
(생신 축하드려요, 할머니! 이 카드는 할머니 거예요.)
W: Oh, thank you. (오, 고맙구나.)
G: You're welcome. (천만에요.)

2 G: Thank you for coming to my party.
(파티에 와줘서 고마워.)
B: Sure. This hat is for you.
(천만에. 이 모자는 네 거야.)
G: Oh, thank you. Would you like some cake?
(오, 고마워. 케이크 좀 먹을래?)
B: Yes, please. (응, 줘.)

3 G: Happy birthday, Ted! This present is for you. (생일 축하해, Ted! 이 선물은 네 거야.)
B: What a surprise! What is it?
(놀랍구나! 이거 뭐야?)
G: Open it. (열어봐.)
B: Oh, I like this robot. Thanks a lot.
(오, 이 로봇 맘에 들어. 정말 고마워.)
G: My pleasure. (천만에.)

P.66~67 **UNIT TEST**

1 ⓐ present (선물) ⓑ backpack (배낭)
ⓒ card (카드) ⓓ robot (로봇)

2 B: Thank you for coming to my party.
(파티에 와줘서 고마워.)
G: This robot is for you. (이 로봇은 네 거야.)
B: Oh, thank you. (오, 고마워.)

3 B: I have a surprise present for you. Open it.
(널 위한 깜짝 선물이야. 열어봐.)
G: Oh, it's a hat. How nice! (오, 모자구나. 좋다!)

Question: Which one is the present for the girl?
(소녀를 위한 선물은 어느 것인가?)

4 W: Would you like some cake? (케이크 좀 먹을래?)
ⓐ What a surprise! (놀랍구나!)

ⓑ This is for you. (이건 네 거야.)

ⓒ You're welcome. (천만에.)

ⓓ Yes, please. (응, 줘.)

5 ⓐ G: Happy birthday! (생일 축하해!)
B: Thank you. (고마워.)
ⓑ G: Thank you for coming. (와줘서 고마워.)
B: My pleasure. (천만에.)
ⓒ G: Would you like some juice? (주스 좀 마실래?)
B: Sure. Thanks. (응. 고마워.)
ⓓ G: Help yourself. (많이 먹어.)
B: You're welcome. (천만에.)

6 W: Happy birthday! This card is for you.
(생일 축하해! 이 카드는 네 거란다.)
G: Thanks, Mom. (고마워요, 엄마.)
M: Happy birthday! This backpack is for you.
(생일 축하해! 이 배낭은 네 거란다.)
G: Oh, it's so pretty. Thanks a lot, Dad.
(오, 너무 예뻐요. 정말 고마워요, 아빠.)

Question: Which present does Dad give?
(아빠가 주는 선물은 어느 것인가?)

7 B: Happy birthday! This hat is for you, Grandma!
(생신 축하드려요! 이 모자는 할머니 거예요!)
W: Oh, thank you. (오, 고맙다.)
B: You're welcome. (천만에요.)
W: Would you like some cake? (케이크 좀 먹을래?)
B: Yes, please. Thank you. (네, 주세요. 감사해요.)

Question: What will the boy's grandma give to him?
(소년의 할머니는 그에게 무엇을 줄 것인가?)

UNIT 8 OUTDOOR ACTIVITIES

ANSWERS

P.68

P.69

P.70

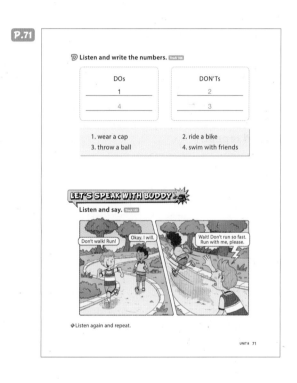

P.71

P.72~73

DICTATION

A 1 t, h   2 s, w   3 s, h
   4 e, a   5 c, h

B 1 run   2 careful   3 ride
   4 Climb   5 jump

C
1 Wear, will
2 throw, sorry
3 swim, friends
4 Watch, out, won't

P.74~75 **UNIT TEST**

1 ⓐ   2 ⓒ   3 ⓑ   4 ⓒ
5 ⓓ   6 ⓑ   7 ⓓ

SCRIPTS & 해석

P.68 **ARE YOU READY?**

⚡ **Listen and number.**

1 **W:** Swim with your brother.
(동생과 함께 수영하렴.)
G: Okay, Mom. (네, 엄마.)

2 **G:** Oops! I'm sorry. (어이쿠! 미안해.)
B: Watch out! Don't run here.
(조심해! 여기서 뛰지 마.)

3 **M:** Climb up the ladder one by one, please.
(한 명씩 사다리를 올라가세요.)
B: Okay. I will. (네. 그럴게요.)

⭐ **Listen and repeat.**

swim (수영하다)   ride ((탈것에) 타다)
catch (잡다)   throw (던지다)
climb up (오르다)   push (밀다)
wear (입다, 쓰다)

P.69 **START UP**

Ⓐ **Listen and number.**

1 swim (수영하다)
2 throw (던지다)
3 climb up (오르다)
4 ride ((탈것에) 타다)

Ⓑ **Listen and match.**

1 **W:** Wear your helmet. (헬멧을 쓰렴.)
B: Okay. (네.)

2 **G:** Don't push me! (날 밀지 마!)
B: I'm sorry. (미안해.)

3 **M:** Don't swim alone. (혼자 수영하지 말거라.)

G: I won't. (안 그럴게요.)

P.69 **SOUND SOUND**

🔘 **Listen and say.**

/ʃ/ push (밀다)   wash (씻다)   brush (붓)
/tʃ/ catch (잡다)   watch (보다; 손목시계)
match (어울리다, 연결하다)

➕ **Listen and circle.**

1 wash   2 watch   3 brush

P.70~71 **LISTEN UP**

Ⓐ **Listen and number.**

1 **G:** Hey! Don't ride your bike here.
(얘! 여기서 자전거 타지 마.)
B: Oh, I'm sorry. I won't. (오, 미안해. 안 그럴게.)

2 **B:** Amy! Catch this ball! (Amy! 이 공을 잡아!)
G: Okay. Throw it here! (응. 여기로 던져!)

3 **W:** Swim with your friends.
(친구들과 함께 수영하렴.)
G: Okay. I will. (네. 그럴게요.)

Ⓑ **Listen and check.**

1 **B:** Run fast! (빨리 뛰어!)
G: Oh, I can't. (이런, 난 못하겠어.)
B: Come on! You can do it! (힘내! 넌 할 수 있어!)

2 **B:** Don't jump into the water. It's dangerous!
(물속으로 뛰어들지 마. 위험해!)
G: Okay. I won't. (응. 안 그럴게.)

3 **M:** Hey! Wear your helmet. (얘야! 헬멧을 쓰렴.)
G: Okay. I will. (네. 그럴게요.)
M: Have fun. (재미있게 놀거라.)

4 **B:** Oops. I'm sorry. Are you okay?
(어이쿠. 죄송합니다. 괜찮으세요?)
M: I'm okay. But don't throw the ball here
again.
(괜찮아. 하지만 다시는 여기서 공을 던지지 말거라.)
B: Okay. I won't. (네. 안 그럴게요.)

Ⓒ **Listen and check.**

1 **B:** Hey! Are you ready? (얘! 준비됐어?)
G: Yes! (응!)
B: Here we go! Catch the ball!
(자, 간다! 공을 잡아!)

G: I will! (그렇게!)

Question: The boy will catch the ball.
(소년은 공을 잡을 것이다.)

2 B: Don't push me! Let's climb up the ladder
one by one.
(날 밀지 마! 한 명씩 사다리를 올라가자.)
G: Oh, I'm sorry. (오, 미안해.)
B: Be careful next time. (다음에는 조심해.)
G: Okay. (알겠어.)

Question: The kids will climb up the ladder
one by one.
(아이들은 한 명씩 사다리를 올라갈 것이다.)

D Listen and write the numbers.

1 G: Hey! Wear your cap. (얘! 모자를 써.)
B: Okay. I will. (응. 그럴게.)

2 W: Watch out! Don't ride your bike in the
street. (조심해! 도로에서 자전거 타지 말거라.)
B: Okay. I won't. (네. 안 그럴게요.)
W: Don't forget. (잊지 말거라.)

3 W: Don't throw the ball here.
(여기서 공을 던지지 말거라.)
G: Oh, I'm sorry. (오, 죄송합니다.)
W: That's okay. But be careful next time.
(괜찮아. 하지만 다음에는 조심하렴.)

4 G: May I swim in the pool?
(수영장에서 수영해도 돼요?)
M: Sure. Swim with your friends.
(물론이지. 친구들과 함께 수영하렴.)
G: Okay. I will. (네. 그럴게요.)

P.71 **LET'S SPEAK WITH BUDDY**

Listen and say.

Jack: Don't walk! Run! (걷지 마! 뛰어!)
Tom: Okay. I will. (응. 그럴게.)

Jack: Wait! Don't run so fast. Run with me, please.
(기다려! 너무 빨리 뛰지 마. 제발 나랑 같이 뛰어.)

P.72~73 **DICTATION**

A 1 throw (던지다)
2 swim (수영하다)
3 push (밀다)
4 wear (입다, 쓰다)

5 catch (잡다)

B 1 Don't run here. (여기서 뛰지 마.)
2 Be careful next time. (다음에는 조심해.)
3 Don't ride your bike here. (여기서 자전거 타지 마.)
4 Climb up the ladder one by one.
(한 명씩 사다리를 올라가렴.)
5 Don't jump into the water. (물속으로 뛰어들지 마.)

C 1 M: Hey! Wear your helmet. (얘야! 헬멧을 쓰렴.)
G: Okay. I will. (네. 그럴게요.)

2 W: Don't throw the ball here.
(여기서 공을 던지지 말거라.)
G: Oh, I'm sorry. (오, 죄송합니다.)

3 G: May I swim in the pool?
(수영장에서 수영해도 돼요?)
M: Sure. Swim with your friends.
(물론이지. 친구들과 함께 수영하렴.)
G: Okay. I will. (네. 그럴게요.)

4 W: Watch out! Don't ride your bike in the
street. (조심해! 도로에서 자전거 타지 말거라.)
B: Okay. I won't. (네. 안 그럴게요.)
W: Don't forget. (잊지 말거라.)

P.74~75 **UNIT TEST**

1 ⓐ catch (잡다)   ⓑ wear (입다, 쓰다)
ⓒ swim (수영하다)   ⓓ push (밀다)

2 ⓐ Don't run so fast. (너무 빨리 뛰지 마.)
ⓑ Don't ride your bike here. (여기서 자전거 타지 마.)
ⓒ Hey! Wear your helmet. (얘! 헬멧을 써.)
ⓓ Climb up the ladder one by one.
(한 명씩 사다리를 올라가.)

3 B: Oops! I'm sorry. (어이쿠! 죄송합니다.)
M: Don't throw the ball here again.
(다시는 여기서 공을 던지지 말거라.)
B: Okay. I won't. (네. 안 그럴게요.)

4 W: Watch out! (조심해!)
B: Oh, I'm sorry. Are you okay?
(오, 죄송합니다. 괜찮으세요?)
W: _____
ⓐ Okay. I will. (응. 그럴게.)
ⓑ Okay. I won't. (응. 안 그럴게.)
ⓒ I'm okay. But be careful next time.
(난 괜찮아. 하지만 다음에는 조심하렴.)
ⓓ Oh, I'm sorry. (오, 미안하구나.)

5 ⓐ **G**: Don't push me. (날 밀지 마.)
   B: Oh, I'm sorry. (오, 미안해.)
 ⓑ **G**: Swim with your friends. (친구들과 함께 수영해.)
   B: Okay. I will. (응. 그럴게.)
 ⓒ **G**: Don't run so fast! (너무 빨리 뛰지 마!)
   B: Okay. I won't. (응. 안 그럴게.)
 ⓓ **G**: Climb up the ladder one by one.
      (한 명씩 사다리를 올라가.)
   B: I'm okay. (난 괜찮아.)

6 **G**: Are you ready? Catch the ball! (*pause*) Oops.
   I'm sorry. (준비됐니? 공을 잡아! 어이쿠. 미안해.)
 B: That's okay. Throw it again.
   (괜찮아. 공을 다시 던져.)
 G: Okay. I will. (응. 그럴게.)

 Question: What are they doing?
          (그들은 무엇을 하고 있는가?)

7 **B**: Mom, may I swim in the pool?
   (엄마, 수영장에서 수영해도 돼요?)
 W: Sure. (*pause*) Oh, don't run near the pool. It's
   dangerous!
   (물론이지. 오, 수영장 근처에서 뛰지 말거라. 위험하단
   다!)
 B: Okay. I won't. (네. 안 그럴게요.)
 W: And swim with your friends.
   (그리고 친구들과 함께 수영하렴.)
 B: Okay. I will. (네. 그럴게요.)

 Question: What will the boy do?
          (소년은 무엇을 할 것인가?)
 ⓐ He will run near the pool.
   (그는 수영장 근처에서 뛰어다닐 것이다.)
 ⓑ He will climb up the ladder.
   (그는 사다리를 올라갈 것이다.)
 ⓒ He will jump into the water.
   (그는 물속으로 뛰어들 것이다.)
 ⓓ He will swim with his friends.
   (그는 친구들과 함께 수영할 것이다.)

ANSWERS

P.76

P.77

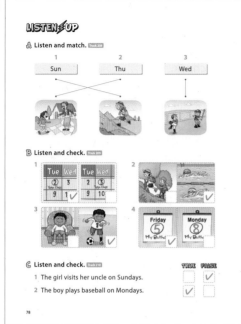

C
1 Thursdays, visits
2 Tuesday, yoga, class
3 What, day, Wednesdays, baseball

P.82~83 UNIT TEST

1 ⓑ 2 ⓐ 3 ⓒ 4 ⓒ
5 ⓐ 6 ⓑ 7 ⓓ

SCRIPTS & 해석

P.76 ARE YOU READY?

⚡ **Listen and number.**
1 G: What day is it today? (오늘 무슨 요일이니?)
   B: It's Wednesday. I play soccer today.
   (수요일이야. 난 오늘 축구를 해.)

2 G: What do you do on Fridays?
   (너는 금요일에 무엇을 하니?)
   B: I play the violin on Fridays.
   (나는 금요일에 바이올린을 연주해.)

3 G: What do you do on Sundays?
   (너는 일요일에 무엇을 하니?)
   B: I go hiking. (나는 등산을 가.)

⭐ **Listen and repeat.**
Sunday (일요일)   Monday (월요일)
Tuesday (화요일)   Wednesday (수요일)
Thursday (목요일)   Friday (금요일)
Saturday (토요일)

play soccer (축구를 하다)
go hiking (등산을 가다)
have a yoga class (요가 수업을 듣다)
visit my uncle (삼촌 댁을 방문하다)

P.77 START UP

A Listen and check.
1 Monday (월요일)
2 Saturday (토요일)
3 Tuesday (화요일)

B Listen and match.
1 B: What do you do on Thursdays?
   (너는 목요일에 무엇을 하니?)
   G: I have a yoga class. (난 요가 수업을 들어.)

P.80~81 DICTATION

A 1 F   2 o   3 u, e, s
    4 d, n   5 t, u, r

B 1 day   2 Thursdays   3 Sundays
    4 hiking   5 weekends

2 G: What does he do on Fridays?
(그는 금요일에 무엇을 하나요?)
W: He plays soccer. (그는 축구를 한다.)

3 B: What day is it today? (오늘 무슨 요일이니?)
G: It's Wednesday. (수요일이야.)

P.77 **SOUND SOUND**

⬡ **Listen and say.**

Silent D Wednesday (수요일) handsome (잘생긴)
sandwich (샌드위치)
○ What day is it today? (오늘 무슨 요일이니?)
○ What do you do on Sundays?
(너는 일요일에 무엇을 하니?)

P.78~79 **LISTEN UP**

Ⓐ **Listen and match.**

1 G: What do you do on Sundays?
(너는 일요일에 무엇을 하니?)
B: I go hiking. (나는 등산을 가.)

2 G: What does she do on Thursdays?
(그녀는 목요일에 무엇을 하니?)
B: She visits her grandmother.
(그녀는 할머니 댁을 방문해.)

3 G: What do they do on Wednesdays?
(그들은 수요일에 무엇을 하니?)
B: They play baseball. (그들은 야구를 해.)

Ⓑ **Listen and check.**

1 W: What day is it today? (오늘 무슨 요일이에요?)
M: It's Tuesday. (화요일이에요.)
W: Oh, I have a yoga class today. I'm late!
(오, 저는 오늘 요가 수업을 들어요. 늦었네요!)

2 G: What do you do on Wednesdays?
(너는 수요일에 무엇을 하니?)
B: I go swimming with my brother.
(나는 내 남동생과 수영하러 가.)
G: Sounds fun. (재미있겠다.)

3 G: What do you do on weekends?
(너는 주말에 무엇을 하니?)
B: I play soccer on weekends.
(나는 주말에 축구를 해.)
G: Can I join you? (같이 해도 돼?)

4 B: What day is it today? (오늘 무슨 요일이니?)

G: It's Friday. Today is my birthday!
(금요일이야. 오늘 내 생일이야!)
B: Oh! Happy birthday! (오! 생일 축하해!)

Ⓒ **Listen and check.**

1 B: What do you do on Sundays?
(너는 일요일에 무엇을 하니?)
G: I go hiking on Sundays. How about you?
(나는 일요일에 등산을 가. 너는 어때?)
B: I visit my uncle. (나는 삼촌 댁을 방문해.)
G: That sounds nice. (좋겠다.)

Question: The girl visits her uncle on Sundays.
(소녀는 일요일에 삼촌 댁을 방문한다.)

2 G: What day is it today? (오늘 무슨 요일이니?)
B: It's Monday. (월요일이야.)
G: What do you do on Mondays?
(너는 월요일에 무엇을 하니?)
B: I play baseball with my friends.
(나는 친구들과 야구를 해.)
G: Can I join you? (같이 해도 돼?)
B: Sure. (물론이지.)

Question: The boy plays baseball on Mondays.
(소년은 월요일에 야구를 한다.)

Ⓓ **Listen and write the numbers.**

B: Amy, are you free today?
(Amy, 너 오늘 시간 있니?)
G: Oh, I'm sorry. I have an art class on Tuesdays.
(오, 미안해. 나는 화요일에는 미술 수업을 들어.)
B: What do you do on Thursdays?
(목요일에는 무엇을 하니?)
G: I play the piano on Thursdays.
(목요일에는 피아노를 연주해.)
B: Then, how about weekends? (그럼, 주말은 어때?)
G: I go hiking on Saturdays and visit my aunt on
Sundays.
(나는 토요일에는 등산을 가고, 일요일에는 이모 댁을 방
문해.)
B: Wow! You're very busy. (와! 너 정말 바쁘구나.)

P.79 **LET'S SPEAK WITH BUDDY**

⬡ **Listen and say.**

Ann: Hey, what day is it today?
(얘, 오늘 무슨 요일이니?)
Jack: It's Friday. (금요일이야.)

Ann: What do you do on Fridays?
(너는 금요일에 무엇을 하니?)

Jack: I visit my uncle on Fridays.
(나는 금요일에 삼촌 댁을 방문해.)

Jack: Oh, no! I have to go now.
(오, 이런! 난 지금 가봐야 해.)

DICTATION

A Listen and write the letters.

1 Friday (금요일)
2 Monday (월요일)
3 Tuesday (화요일)
4 Wednesday (수요일)
5 Saturday (토요일)

B Listen and write the words.

1 What day is it today? (오늘 무슨 요일이니?)
2 I visit my uncle on Thursdays.
(나는 목요일에 삼촌 댁을 방문해.)
3 What do you do on Sundays?
(너는 일요일에 무엇을 하니?)
4 They go hiking on Saturdays.
(그들은 토요일에 등산을 가.)
5 I play soccer on weekends.
(나는 주말에 축구를 해.)

C Listen and fill in the blanks.

1 G: What does she do on Thursdays?
(그녀는 목요일에 무엇을 하니?)
B: She visits her grandmother.
(그녀는 할머니 댁을 방문해.)

2 W: What day is it today? (오늘 무슨 요일이에요?)
M: It's Tuesday. (화요일이에요.)
W: Oh, I have a yoga class today. I'm late!
(오, 저는 오늘 요가 수업을 들어요. 늦었네요!)

3 G: What day is it today? (오늘 무슨 요일이니?)
B: It's Wednesday. (수요일이야.)
G: What do you do on Wednesdays?
(너는 수요일에 무엇을 하니?)
B: I play baseball with my friends.
(나는 친구들과 야구를 해.)
G: Can I join you? (같이 해도 돼?)
B: Sure. (물론이지.)

UNIT TEST

1 ⓐ Monday (월요일)　　ⓑ Tuesday (화요일)
ⓒ Thursday (목요일)　ⓓ Friday (금요일)

2 ⓐ He goes hiking on Saturdays.
(그는 토요일에 등산을 간다.)
ⓑ He plays soccer on Saturdays.
(그는 토요일에 축구를 한다.)
ⓒ He goes hiking on Sundays.
(그는 일요일에 등산을 간다.)
ⓓ He plays soccer on Sundays.
(그는 일요일에 축구를 한다.)

3 G: What do you do on Fridays?
(너는 금요일에 무엇을 하니?)
B: I have an art class. (나는 미술 수업을 들어.)

Question: What does the boy do on Fridays?
(소년은 금요일에 무엇을 하는가?)

4 B: What does she do on Mondays?
(그녀는 월요일에 무엇을 하니?)
ⓐ It's Sunday. (일요일이야.)
ⓑ I have a yoga class on Mondays.
(나는 월요일에 요가 수업을 들어.)
ⓒ She plays the violin. (그녀는 바이올린을 연주해.)
ⓓ No, she doesn't. (아니, 그녀는 하지 않아.)

5 ⓐ B: What day is it? (무슨 요일이니?)
G: It's the weekend. (주말이야.)
ⓑ B: What do you do on Thursdays?
(너는 목요일에 무엇을 하니?)
G: I have an art class. (나는 미술 수업을 들어.)
ⓒ B: What does your father do on Sundays?
(너희 아빠는 일요일에 무엇을 하시니?)
G: He goes hiking. (그는 등산을 가셔.)
ⓓ B: What day is it today? (오늘 무슨 요일이니?)
G: It's Friday. (금요일이야.)

6 G: Josh, what do you do on Mondays?
(Josh, 너는 월요일에 무엇을 하니?)
B: I go swimming on Mondays.
(나는 월요일에 수영하러 가.)
G: What about Wednesdays? (수요일은?)
B: I have a math class. Oh, today is Wednesday.
I'm late!
(수학 수업을 들어. 오, 오늘이 수요일이네. 늦었어!)

Question: What day is it today?
(오늘은 무슨 요일인가?)

7 B: I play soccer today. Are you free?
(나는 오늘 축구를 해. 너 시간 있니?)
G: What day is it today? (오늘 무슨 요일이니?)
B: It's Thursday. (목요일이야.)
G: Oh, I'm sorry. I visit my grandfather on
Thursdays.

(오, 미안해. 나는 목요일에는 할아버지 댁을 방문해.)
B: It's okay. Have fun! (괜찮아. 즐거운 시간 보내!)

Question: The girl <u>visits her grandfather</u> on
Thursdays.
(소녀는 목요일에 <u>할아버지 댁을 방문한다</u>.)

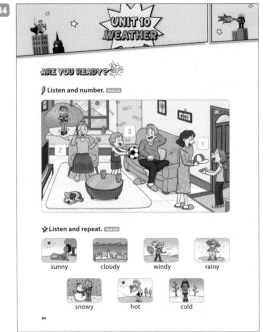

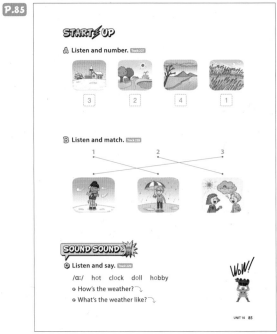

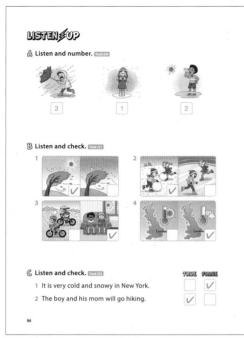

LISTEN UP

A Listen and number. `Track 210`

3   1   2

B Listen and check. `Track 211`

1 ✓ (left)

2 ✓ (right)

3 ✓ (right)

4 ✓ (right)

C Listen and check. `Track 212`

	TRUE	FALSE
1 It is very cold and snowy in New York.		✓
2 The boy and his mom will go hiking.	✓	

86

D Listen and write. `Track 213`

ⓐ ⓑ

ⓒ ⓓ

1 Sue's Diary ⓑ

2 Joe's Diary ⓓ

LET'S SPEAK WITH BUDDY

Listen and say. `Track 214`

Let's ride our bikes.

How's the weather today, Dad?

It's rainy and cold.

Let's just stay at home.

We can ride this bike!

↻ Listen again and repeat.

UNIT 10 87

DICTATION

A 1 o   2 w   3 n, n
4 a, i   5 o, u

B 1 weather   2 snowy   3 cold
4 Let's   5 like

C 1 How's, cloudy
2 sunny, go, out
3 warm, go, swimming, great

UNIT TEST

1 ⓓ   2 ⓓ   3 ⓑ   4 ⓒ
5 ⓓ   6 ⓑ   7 ⓒ

SCRIPTS & 해석

ARE YOU READY?

⚡ **Listen and number.**

1 **G**: Mom, what's the weather like?
(엄마, 날씨 어때요?)
W: It's sunny. Wear your cap. (화창해. 모자 쓰렴.)

2 **W**: How's the weather there? (거기 날씨 어떠니?)
G: It's very cold. (너무 추워요.)

3 **B**: The weather is so nice. Let's play soccer outside.
(날씨가 정말 좋아요. 밖에서 축구 해요.)
M: Sorry. I'm tired. (미안하다. 피곤하구나.)

☆ **Listen and repeat.**

sunny (화창한)   cloudy (흐린, 구름이 많은)
windy (바람이 부는)   rainy (비가 오는)
snowy (눈이 오는)   hot (더운)
cold (추운)

START UP

A Listen and number.

1 windy (바람이 부는)
2 sunny (화창한)
3 snowy (눈이 오는)
4 cloudy (흐린, 구름이 많은)

B Listen and match.

1 **G**: How's the weather there? (거기 날씨 어때?)
B: It's rainy. (비가 와.)

2 **B**: It's hot today. Let's go swimming.
(오늘 덥다. 수영하러 가자.)
G: That's a good idea. (좋은 생각이야.)

37

3 **B**: What's the weather like there?
  (거기 날씨 어때?)
  G: It's so cold. (너무 추워.)

P.85 **SOUND SOUND**

🔊 Listen and say.

/ɑː/ hot (더운) clock (시계)
  doll (인형) hobby (취미)
 ◦ How's the weather? (날씨 어때?)
 ◦ What's the weather like? (날씨 어때?)

P.86~87 **LISTEN UP**

A Listen and number.

1 **B**: What's the weather like? (날씨 어때?)
  G: It's snowy and cold. (눈이 오고 추워.)

2 **G**: How's the weather today? (오늘 날씨 어때?)
  B: It's sunny and hot. (화창하고 더워.)

3 **G**: What's the weather like there?
  (거기 날씨 어때?)
  B: It's rainy and windy. (비가 오고 바람이 불어.)

B Listen and check.

1 **G**: What's the weather like today?
  (오늘 날씨 어때?)
  B: It's sunny but windy. (화창하지만 바람이 불어.)
  G: Let's go out. (밖에 나가자.)
  B: No, let's not. (아니, 그러지 말자.)

2 **B**: How's the weather? (날씨 어때?)
  G: It's snowy. (눈이 와.)
  B: Great! Let's make a snowman.
  (좋아! 눈사람 만들자.)
  G: Sounds fun! (재미있겠다!)

3 **B**: Julie, let's ride our bikes. (Julie, 자전거 타자.)
  G: Sorry. It's very hot outside. Let's read books
  at home.
  (미안해. 밖에 너무 더워. 집에서 책 읽자.)
  B: Sounds good. (좋아.)

4 **W**: How's the weather in London?
  (런던의 날씨는 어떠니?)
  B: It's cloudy and cold. (흐리고 추워요.)
  W: Oh, dress warmly. (오, 따뜻하게 입으럼.)

C Listen and check.

1 **G**: How's the weather in New York?
  (뉴욕의 날씨는 어때?)
  B: It's rainy. How's the weather in Seoul?
  (비가 와. 서울의 날씨는 어때?)
  G: It's very cold and snowy. (너무 춥고 눈이 와.)
  B: Oh, stay warm. (오, 따뜻하게 하고 있어.)
  G: Okay. Thanks. (알았어. 고마워.)

  Question: It is very cold and snowy in New
  York.
  (뉴욕은 매우 춥고 눈이 온다.)

2 **B**: Mom, what's the weather like?
  (엄마, 날씨 어때요?)
  W: It's sunny. (화창해.)
  B: Is it hot? (더워요?)
  W: No, it's cool. (아니, 시원해.)
  B: Good! Let's go hiking. (좋네요! 등산 가요.)
  W: That's a good idea. (좋은 생각이구나.)

  Question: The boy and his mom will go
  hiking.
  (소년과 그의 엄마는 등산을 갈 것이다.)

D Listen and write.

1 **B**: Sue, how's the weather today?
  (Sue, 오늘 날씨 어때?)
  G: It's sunny and warm. (화창하고 따뜻해.)
  B: Let's go swimming. (수영하러 가자.)
  G: Sorry, but I can't swim. How about riding
  our bikes?
  (미안하지만, 난 수영을 못해. 자전거 타는 게 어때?)
  B: Sounds great. (좋아.)

2 **G**: Joe, I'm bored. Let's play soccer.
  (Joe, 나 심심해. 축구하자.)
  B: Look outside. It's rainy. (밖을 봐. 비가 와.)
  G: Oh, then let's read books at home.
  (오, 그럼 집에서 책 읽자.)
  B: Okay, let's do that. (좋아, 그렇게 하자.)

P.87 **LET'S SPEAK WITH BUDDY**

🔊 Listen and say.

Kevin: Let's ride our bikes. (자전거 타자.)

Ann: How's the weather today, Dad?
  (아빠, 오늘 날씨 어때요?)
Dad: It's rainy and cold. (비가 오고 추워.)

Ann: Let's just stay at home. (그냥 집에 있자.)

Kevin: We can ride this bike!
(우리 이 자전거를 탈 수 있어!)

P.88~89 **DICTATION**

A 1 hot (더운)
2 windy (바람이 부는)
3 sunny (화창한)
4 rainy (비가 오는)
5 cloudy (흐린, 구름이 많은)

B 1 How's the weather today? (오늘 날씨 어때?)
2 It's snowy. (눈이 와.)
3 Is it cold? (추워?)
4 Let's ride our bikes. (자전거 타자.)
5 What's the weather like? (날씨 어때?)

C 1 **W:** How's the weather in London?
(런던의 날씨는 어떠니?)
B: It's cloudy and cold. (흐리고 추워요.)
W: Oh, dress warmly. (오, 따뜻하게 입으렴.)

2 **G:** What's the weather like today?
(오늘 날씨 어때?)
B: It's sunny but windy. (화창하지만 바람이 불어.)
G: Let's go out. (밖에 나가자.)
B: No, let's not. (아니, 그러지 말자.)

3 **B:** Sue, how's the weather today?
(Sue, 오늘 날씨 어때?)
G: It's sunny and warm. (화창하고 따뜻해.)
B: Let's go swimming. (수영하러 가자.)
G: Sorry, but I can't swim. How about riding
our bikes?
(미안하지만, 난 수영을 못해. 자전거 타는 게 어때?)
B: Sounds great. (좋아.)

W: No, it's warm. (아니, 따뜻해.)

4 **B:** It's hot and sunny today. Let's go swimming.
(오늘 덥고 화창하다. 수영하러 가자.)
ⓐ Okay, let's not. (그래, 그러지 말자.)
ⓑ Yes, it is. (응, 그렇네.)
ⓒ Sounds great. (좋아.)
ⓓ Oh, dress warmly. (오, 따뜻하게 입어.)

5 ⓐ **G:** What's the weather like there?
(거기 날씨 어때?)
B: It's cloudy. (흐려.)
ⓑ **G:** Is it hot? (더워?)
B: No, it's cool. (아니, 시원해.)
ⓒ **G:** Let's ride our bikes. (자전거 타자.)
B: Sorry. I'm tired. (미안해. 나 피곤해.)
ⓓ **G:** How's the weather today? (오늘 날씨 어때?)
B: Okay. Let's go out. (그래. 밖에 나가자.)

6 **G:** David, let's play soccer. (David, 축구하자.)
B: It's too hot outside. (밖에 너무 더워.)
G: Oh, really? (이런, 정말?)
B: Yes, let's go swimming. (응, 수영하러 가자.)
G: Oh, that's a good idea. (오, 좋은 생각이야.)

Question: What will they do?
(그들은 무엇을 할 것인가?)

7 **G:** How's the weather in New York?
(뉴욕의 날씨는 어때요?)
M: It's sunny but windy. How's the weather in
London?
(화창하지만 바람이 불어. 런던의 날씨는 어때?)
G: It's cloudy and cold. (흐리고 추워요.)
M: Oh, dress warmly. (오, 따뜻하게 입으렴.)
G: Okay, thanks. (알았어요, 감사해요.)

Question: How's the weather in London?
(런던의 날씨는 어떠한가?)

P.90~91 **UNIT TEST**

1 ⓐ rainy (비가 오는)　　ⓑ sunny (화창한)
ⓒ windy (바람이 부는)　ⓓ snowy (눈이 오는)

2 ⓐ It's sunny and hot. (화창하고 덥다.)
ⓑ It's rainy and cold. (비가 오고 춥다.)
ⓒ It's cloudy and hot. (흐리고 덥다.)
ⓓ It's windy and cold. (바람이 불고 춥다.)

3 **B:** How's the weather in Seoul, Grandma?
(할머니, 서울의 날씨는 어때요?)
W: It's rainy. (비가 온단다.)
B: Is it cold? (추워요?)

P.92~93
REVIEW TEST 3 UNITS 7~10

| 1 ⓑ | 2 ⓒ | 3 ⓐ | 4 ⓑ | 5 ⓒ |
| 6 ⓓ | 7 ⓒ | 8 ⓒ | 9 ⓒ | 10 ⓓ |

1 ⓐ push (밀다)　　ⓑ throw (던지다)
ⓒ ride ((탈것에) 타다)　ⓓ wear (입다, 쓰다)

2 ⓐ cloudy (흐린, 구름이 많은)　ⓑ windy (바람이 부는)
ⓒ rainy (비가 오는)　　　　　ⓓ snowy (눈이 오는)

3 W: Happy birthday! This present is for you.
       (생일 축하해! 이 선물은 네 거란다.)
   B: What a surprise! What is it?
       (놀라워요! 이거 뭐예요?)
   W: Open it. (열어보렴.)
   B: Oh, I like this backpack. Thank you, Mom.
       (오, 이 배낭 맘에 들어요. 감사해요, 엄마.)

4 G: Are you free today? (너 오늘 시간 있니?)
   B: What day is it today? (오늘 무슨 요일이니?)
   G: _____
   ⓐ Yes, it is. (응, 맞아.)
   ⓑ It's Wednesday. (수요일이야.)
   ⓒ You're very busy. (너는 정말 바쁘구나.)
   ⓓ I go hiking on Fridays. (나는 금요일에 등산을 가.)

5 G: What's the weather like? (날씨 어때?)
   B: It's sunny. (화창해.)
   G: Is it hot? (더워?)
   B: _____
   ⓐ Yes, it's windy. (응, 바람이 불어.)
   ⓑ Sorry. I'm tired. (미안해. 나 피곤해.)
   ⓒ No, it's cool. (아니, 시원해.)
   ⓓ That's a good idea. (좋은 생각이야.)

6 ⓐ B: Would you like some cake? (케이크 좀 먹을래?)
       G: Yes, thank you. (응, 고마워.)
   ⓑ B: What do you do on Tuesdays?
       (너는 화요일에 무엇을 하니?)
       G: I have a yoga class. (나는 요가 수업을 들어.)
   ⓒ B: Don't jump into the water.
       (물속으로 뛰어들지 마.)
       G: Okay, I won't. (응, 안 그럴게.)
   ⓓ B: How's the weather today? (오늘 날씨 어때?)
       G: Oh, then let's go swimming.
       (오, 그럼 수영하러 가자.)

7 ⓐ G: Thank you for coming. (와줘서 고마워.)
       B: My pleasure. Help yourself.
       (천만에. 많이 먹어.)
   ⓑ G: Oops, I'm sorry. Are you okay?
       (어이쿠, 미안해. 괜찮니?)
       B: I'm okay. But be careful next time.
       (난 괜찮아. 하지만 다음에는 조심해.)
   ⓒ G: What day is it today? (오늘 무슨 요일이니?)
       B: It's Monday. Today is my birthday.
       (월요일이야. 오늘 내 생일이야.)
   ⓓ G: It's snowy. Let's make a snowman.
       (눈이 와. 눈사람 만들자.)
       B: Okay, let's do that. (좋아, 그렇게 하자.)

8 B: Hello, Amy. How's the weather there?

       (안녕, Amy. 거기 날씨 어때?)
   G: It's rainy. How's the weather there?
       (비가 와. 거기 날씨는 어때?)
   B: It's very cold and snowy. (너무 춥고 눈이 와.)
   G: Oh, stay warm. (오, 따뜻하게 하고 있어.)
   B: Okay. Thanks. (응. 고마워.)
   Question: Where does the boy live?
       (소년은 어디에 사는가?)

9 G: Dad, may I ride my bike?
       (아빠, 자전거 타도 돼요?)
   M: Sure, but don't ride your bike in the street.
       It's dangerous.
       (물론이지, 하지만 도로에서 타지 말거라. 위험하단다.)
   G: Okay. I won't. (네. 안 그럴게요.)
   M: And wear your helmet. (그리고 헬멧을 쓰렴.)
   G: Okay. I will. (네. 그럴게요.)
   M: Be careful and have fun.
       (조심하고 재미있게 놀거라.)
   Question: The girl will wear a helmet.
       (소녀는 헬멧을 쓸 것이다.)

10 G: Are you free today? Let's play baseball!
       (너 오늘 시간 있니? 야구 하자!)
   B: Oh, I'm sorry. I have an art class on Fridays.
       (오, 미안해. 나는 금요일에는 미술 수업을 들어.)
   G: How about weekends? (주말은 어때?)
   B: I go hiking on Saturdays and visit my uncle on
       Sundays.
       (토요일에는 등산을 가고, 일요일에는 삼촌 댁을 방문해.)
   G: Wow! You're very busy. (와! 너는 정말 바쁘구나.)
   Question: The boy visits his uncle on Sundays.
       (소년은 일요일에 삼촌 댁을 방문한다.)

초등학생의 영어 친구
리스닝버디
LISTENING BUDDY 1

★ **리스닝버디의 특징**

- **fun and friendly** 흥미로운 소재로 구성된 쉽고 재미있는 교재
- **step by step** 듣기 실력 향상을 위한 체계적인 구성
- **carefully prepared** 교육부에서 제시한 초등 교과과정의 의사소통 기능 반영
- **authentic language** 실생활에서 활용 가능한 대화 제시
- **productive** 발음 학습 및 speaking 활동을 보강하여 듣기와 말하기의 결합 강화